SONGS *of* ASSENT

Carla A. Waterman

Pamela K. Keske
Illustrator

For Ethan and Allyse

Only where love and need are one,
And the work is play for mortal stakes,
Is the deed ever really done
For Heaven and the future's sakes.

Robert Frost, *Two Tramps in Mud Time*

Contents

Foreword

My first meeting with Carla Waterman was in January of 2001, when she and Reggie Kidd taught the inaugural session of the capstone course, "Sacred Actions and Ministries," in the doctoral program of the Robert E. Webber Institute for Worship Studies. Although I serve there as Dean of the Chapel, I quickly learned I could turn to each of them for spiritual counsel and prayer support in my own life. They have become two of my dearest friends.

From the delightful wordplay of her title, *Songs of Assent*, to her articulation of the quintet of distinctly feminine virtues simplicity, receptivity, wisdom, confidence and buoyancy, Carla Waterman has crafted what should, and I pray will, become a new Christian devotional classic. As the ancient church understood worship to be a "Song of Ascents," a joining of heaven and earth, so this work carries that concept into our daily spirituality, which is only authentic and effective if it is a "song" of repeated "assents" or "yeses" to the Spirit of the living God.

Although this study/meditation focuses on the virtuous qualities of Mary, the mother of Jesus, it is not some soft and sentimental musing based on the prototypical mother; nor is it a strident feminist manifesto. It is far more muscular than the former and infinitely tenderer than the latter.

Resisting typical ambiguity, as well as traditional patriarchal and feminist thought, *Songs of Assent* scandalously embraces the particularity of gender in a strikingly biblical and practical fashion. *Songs of Assent* dares to define the feminine. And what invaluable ground it breaks, for both men and women.

There is much deep, practical spirituality here. We are reminded, "the bearing of fruit is a feminine wonder." We learn of "the solid quiet" of spirit only found by walking this path. We also learn the differences between "receptivity" and "passivity." Dr. Waterman points out that virtually every human language that assigns gender in its nouns, assigns the feminine gender to the human soul. (That would include the masculine soul, as well as the feminine one.)

Carla Waterman also takes a courageous pastoral tack by teaching not just through spiritual, philosophical, intuitive and artistic insight. She also vulnerably shares profoundly intimate stories from her own spiritual journey. These "songs" have not just been contemplated academically but also spiritually, forged in the crucible of daily living.

For any male readers who may wonder, "What's a book on feminine qualities got to do with me?" The answer is, "Everything."

Brothers, we have been baptized into the Body of Christ, and have become members of his Bride for eternity. But we know so little about how to respond to Christ as our Bridegroom; and we need to learn to relate to him that way now and become prepared to relate to him that way throughout all eternity. Dr. Waterman has offered us an invaluable gift of insight into the requisite feminine perspective. Let's begin here and then continue learning from her and our other female siblings, as well.

I hope women will read *Songs of Assent* because it will help them rediscover an authentic femininity that has been maligned, caricatured and sabotaged not just by culture, but so often by the church as well. And I hope men will read *Songs of Assent* so we might better learn how to take our place alongside our sisters as members of a distinctly feminine personage, the Bride of Christ, imbued with simplicity, receptivity, wisdom, confidence and buoyancy.

Darrell A. Harris

Partner,

The Stonebridge Institute

Dean of the Chapel,

The Robert E. Webber Institute for Worship Studies

Acknowledgments

This book has been gestating for many years and while it now breathes on its own, it has by no means been formed alone. There are several key people who have been essential dialogue partners as I have been learning to live and teach what I am coming to understand about receptivity to God in the formation of Christian faith.

My first dialogue partner is my "taller, younger, louder" sister, Pamela Keske. We have been close from the moment she appeared in my five-year-old universe, but a creative collaboration has grown up between us as we have shared what we are learning about Christian formation in everyday life: I teach, she illustrates—whether in story, in song, or now in the pen and ink drawings that form the "folk icons" for this book.

My second dialogue partner is Dr. Reggie Kidd—my teaching partner at the Robert E. Webber Institute for Worship Studies and my spiritual elder brother. Our ongoing collaboration is one of God's delightful surprises. Many of the theological nuances in this book are the fruit of our long conversations inside and outside the classroom during the past eight years.

My third dialogue partner is Valerie McIntyre, my long-time prayer partner and ministry colleague. Valerie's personal support, theological grounding and spiritual sensitivity have been priceless gifts to me in the final stages of writing this book.

I also acknowledge with gratitude my spiritual mentors— Leanne Payne, who walked alongside me in the critically formative years when I was awakening to the wonders of life in Christ, and the late Robert Webber who invested in my life by blessing my vocation, opening doors, shoving me through them, and grinning as he went on to do the next thing. Both Leanne's and Bob's investment in me mark almost every page in this book. I have attempted to credit them, particularly Leanne, as her work so closely influences the themes of this specific book. At the same time, I have found it nearly impossible to footnote these friendships.

I am also thankful for Larry Kochendorfer and Marcy Hintz whose generous readings of the original manuscript at critical points encouraged and strengthened my thinking; and for Darrell Harris whose deep openness to the work-in-progress awakened in me the courage to write. And to the women in the varied seasons of *Women in the Kingdom* at Wheaton College, thank you for the critical gift of questions that needed to be asked.

My colleagues, friends and students over the years at Wheaton College, Church of the Resurrection, Northern Seminary, The Robert E. Webber Institute for Worship Studies and St. John Lutheran Church have offered me treasures now embedded in my heart. I am the beneficiary of God's good gifts through more of his people than I could possibly name. If there are any riches within this book, they have been first tasted in Christian community.

Finally, my husband, Wyatt, has been my consistent rock when everything else human is shaking, and my teenage son, Ethan, has both challenged me to live more deeply in the faith I seek to profess, and rewarded me in ways he cannot yet know as he helps me stay enrolled in Christ's school of wisdom and love. Together, Wyatt and Ethan help me keep life in perspective and remain firmly rooted in the mundane corners of life. Upon consideration, the very daily-ness of life with "my guys" may be one of God's greatest graces—both to my life, and to this book.

Introduction

I'm not fond of the first session of a college class. Any class. I watch from the front as students come in and find a seat. Some of them look around to see if they know anybody. Some just keep their heads down and look occupied. In most classes there is an unsettled restlessness in the room.

But as I began a new season of *Women in the Kingdom,* the room lacked that rustling silence. Each woman was an island unto to herself. I had anticipated this class as a kind of homecoming. A decade prior I had developed this discipleship course for women while on the faculty of Wheaton College. After a nine-year hiatus, I had been invited to return and teach my "signature" course. But the reception at this moment was guarded, at best.

After a few preliminary activities, I offered a bit of my own journey as a woman being formed in faith. I described this journey in terms of a favorite high school youth group activity— tubing down a lazy river with my friends, arms and legs interlocked as we slowly made our way down the river, only to be stopped by a chain-linked fence that protected us from dangerous rapids on the other side. "The Christian conversation about gender looks a lot like my experience on the river. We connect with those with whom we agree on this 'issue' and float down the river together, only to find that we reach a place where we simply can go no further. It is so very easy to find ourselves in treacherous waters without at all being sure how we got there."

And then I threw out the question that cast us all headlong into those precarious waters. "So, what does 'feminine' mean?"

A shocked silence and then quick, sarcastic, bitter words. Pink. Lacy. Blonde. Dumb. I wrote them down.

Our chain link fence quickly became barbed wire. One of my seniors, in great agitation, exclaimed, "I can't believe we are actually saying these things—and that you are writing them down."

And I—blessing the Lord that I was not new to teaching or to this particular content—said, "These are images that reside, unbidden, in our souls when we think of what 'feminine' means. And I am writing them down so we can get them outside ourselves and look at them. You have a right to your strong response. And I have a responsibility to create an environment where we are all safe to look at what emerges the second before we shut the gate in our hearts."

So we were off—on an intense, tearful, joyful adventure of discovering what "feminine" might actually mean and why it matters—not only for the growth of these particular women, but, in the end, for the wellness of every home, workplace and community where their roots will rest.

We were all changed by that first night. Reflecting back, one woman wrote,

> I entered this class with my guard up. Having spent much time studying women in ministry before, I was concerned to hear what was going to be said and how others would respond. My heart was for others to come to the understanding of where I was, with my traditional views and "biblically" based opinions. Oh, how that has been turned upside down. I am

beginning to realize how I was stuck in the quick sand, paralyzed by "dos" and "do nots" rather than living in the freedom of the Lord's blessing upon us as women.

And my passionate senior explained,

As I process back to the first day of class when I shared where I was on the river, I had no idea how much weight and truth I was speaking. I described myself as one who had a perception of being grounded in my ideas regarding gender studies and thus believed myself to be climbing up the fence and ready to jump over. I laugh at myself in realizing how much this class flung me off the fence and back into the bubbling water of ideas, struggling to wrap my hands around a float.

If this class turned one woman's world on its head and knocked her unlikely sister, splashing, back into the water, the same class set my feet firmly on the bank alongside my sisters. Something awoke in me as I watched these young women flounder. They have come of age in a decade of normalized cultural confusion over gender, both outside and inside the church. I do not find it surprising that my students are struggling for ground and gasping for air. In their experience, conversations too quickly turn to battles; sisters become antagonists to be persuaded or abandoned.

There is a single word to describe what was missing in that first session. Wonder. We were missing a startled awe at the profound reality embodied in us as women. Feminine is the greater reality, quietly resting in the depths of a responsive earth, an awakened Christian soul, a church waiting for her bridegroom. And woman? She is the symbol, the thoughtful image bearer of *all* that is responsive in creation. When the splendor of that which is creaturely and dependent on God again fills her being with beauty and meaning then she will regain wonder. And when such wonder is awakened, her soul will begin to sing.

I turned fifty this fall—and I like it. I like the challenge of the brisk wind catching life's autumn leaves as they fall in vibrant pools at one's feet—pools to be stirred into life by laughing children and to be nestled around vulnerable things on their way to winter rest. I like the mellowing of earlier tastes and the savoring of more subtle flavors. I like the freedom to be hidden or visible at the Lord's bidding, to be a willow bending low to the earth and offering shade under which others can come and rest awhile.

And, while I haven't always appreciated the process, I like the result of the wind that has sometimes whipped very hard through my thinking—blowing away the dross firmly entangled around the occasional kernel of a real thought intended to sprout deep roots and live. Over the years I have sought to articulate this uncomfortable experience of thinking as the long, challenging trail from simplistic to complicated to simple.

The process always goes something like this: I get a taste of a great reality, like the incarnation or baptism into Christ or, to the point, the essence of feminine reality. The taste is intoxicating. And, being facile with words and blessed with great dialogue partners, I am rarely at a loss for something to say...at first. The rose is still in bud—full of the promise of goodness. It has yielded a bit of its secret—just enough to captivate me for life.

And then comes a long season where everything gets messy. Even though there is the memory of the taste I once held on my tongue, the memory merely increases the longing. And with longing comes a kind of muteness. I cannot have the initial taste back, but I know both too much and too little to let it go. Here teaching is tinged with terror. The communicator cannot communicate. The large and messy questions shout. The deep responses run and hide.

These are moments when I am completely sympathetic to the temptation to tame "complicated" by creating a recipe— articulating a set of techniques and methods that will attempt to recreate that first illuminating moment. Maybe I can sneak up on it again. Analyze it. Break it down into its component parts. If I can just take an inventory of all the ingredients that went into that first taste, then perhaps I can make it available to others as well. But "complicated" striving always disappoints. For whenever I attempt to frame an analytic consideration of "the nature of feminine," pinning her down like a bug for dissection, I consistently find that she has eluded me, like a woodland nymph who will not be scrutinized. When it comes to such a great thing, any knowledge I seek to generate is merely an artifact of a tasted truth that cannot be replicated on command.

Rather, I have needed to be patient with her, letting that which is feminine speak in her own way. For feminine reality is best understood glimpsed out of the corner of one's eye. She can be tasted in simple stories and great literature, pictured in verbal and visual images, celebrated in poetry and music. She is most beautifully savored in the presence of Christian women who know themselves loved by God, carry his manifold graces deep within, and respond by loving him and their neighbor for his sake.

We miss the deep significance of feminine reality as long as we prize busy-ness over stillness, competition over cooperation, strategic planning over wisdom and immediate success over long-term fruitfulness. And whenever she lies unacknowledged and unappreciated we inevitably grow spiritually barren.

But we are not left orphans. The blessing of all that is feminine has long been received and carried by others. "Here are the three measures of flour, and here is the yeast.[1] Come, let's stir the batter together. Put your hands under mine as we knead the loaf. Let's rest while we watch it rise." Thus we wait together for the warm, fragrant miracle that comes about "perhaps not without our own efforts, but nevertheless not through those efforts."[2]

So, on the far side of dross-sifting storms and nymph-eluding analyses, I want to venture a different response to the question that sent my class spinning. "What does 'feminine' mean?" Simple. Receptive. Wise. Confident. Buoyant. I understand these qualities to be feminine responses to the love of God, and, as such, they frame the contents of this book.[3] Each response, or "song," begins with a folk icon[4] that I will then seek to express in words. We will ponder the unique sound of these embodied antiphons that are intended to well up from our in-graced souls, for renewed spiritual wellness fills us whenever the Holy Spirit pours the Father's rich and relentless grace into hearts made receptive to his love.

This winsome wedding of spiritual wellness with all that is receptive to God, and thus, deeply feminine, has been handed down from generation to generation. But if we would reclaim the spiritual significance of that which is most fundamentally feminine, we would do well to spend time with a mother whose whole life radiated a "habitual availability"[5] to God. For that mother we look to Mary, the mother of our Lord. At the beginning of each chapter we will pause for a moment beside her as we listen to five "songs" through which Mary expresses her assent to God—sometimes in her words, always in her actions.

Mary's songs of assent began as she responded in *simple* trust to an angel's astonishing announcement, expressed as "Let it be to me according to your word." Even as she pondered Elizabeth's proclamation, "Blessed is she who believed," Mary's eyes saw the fruition of God's initiative as it was implanted in her *receptive* heart and womb. Her deeply digested *wisdom* is best witnessed through Mary's song, "My soul magnifies the Lord," and is accompanied by the *confident* recognition of the Lord's protection acquired in the long shadow of "a sword shall pierce your soul." And after thirty years of grace-filled practice, Mary's faith-formed heart rebounded with the moment-by-moment *buoyancy* of her redirected direction in "Do whatever he tells you."

From the beginning, this young woman's in-graced assent to God's utterly unique call revealed "the feminine element in faith [that] is a complete openness and readiness for the 'divine seed' that is to come..."[6] While the Scriptures never directly refer to Mary as the second Eve, it didn't take long for the early church to draw the parallels.[7] Eve had grasped for wisdom in the wrong way and in the wrong time, thwarting God's desire and right to give our first parents what they needed to know when they needed to know it. Mary did not grasp. Instead, she let go.

And yielding all she received everything. God held nothing back—he gave "all of grace to all of Mary."[8] This grace both strengthened the intent of her will and quickened the life in her womb. And Mary, from unfathomable feminine depths, brought forth the world's only hope for wellness.

In this book I have invited Mary to walk alongside us as a very human mentor in a very earthy world, allowing us to see afresh the feminine contours of faith on the days where Gabriel is not conspicuous and the wise men have gone home. For Mary's availability to God is not frozen in a single moment in time. Like all human beings, she is given the choice of her response step by step down the long road between the annunciation and the cross. At every crossroad her renewed reception of God's nuanced grace forms within her the creaturely strength specific to her need. And while "the fruit of her womb" sets her apart as "blessed among women," it is the steady fulfillment of her initial "let it be unto me" throughout her life that puts the period at the end of that proclamation. Perhaps there is no word so pregnantly feminine as "yes."

As our mentor, Mary is also our cantor, the worship leader who sings the solo that gathers the people of God so that we can join our hearts in response. For the better part of this book we will follow her lead and explore how these songs of assent might be sung more deeply in our own lives.

I have written most intimately for my sisters in Christ. I am calling us to "magnanimity"—greatness of soul—that is only to be found through the paradox of Christ's passion. Just as Mary's road led her to the foot of her son's cross, so we, like Mary's companions, are invited to accompany her there. For only as we are caught up in the wake of Jesus' great and final "yes" to the

Father do we find the possibility that our little moments of "yes" can actually be brought forth in the faith-forming corners of our lives.

But as my sisters warm to this topic, I often find brothers who pop up around the corner and tip their ear toward the conversation in progress. Over the past few years they have been listening to tapes and reading lecture notes; they make quiet inquiries. A conversation on the nature of receptivity to God is not a conversation for women only. Every faith-bearing soul is a receptive soul, carrying gifts received from someone else.

And so, while I open my heart to my sisters, I also invite my brothers to pull up a chair and rest for a bit. For the more I discover and embrace the blessing of embodying that which is truly feminine, the more clearly I perceive the spiritual fruit uniquely borne through the men I encounter—my husband and son, my colleagues, friends and students, my living mentors and those whose books line my shelves and sharpen my mind. I am profoundly blessed and strengthened by these men. I taste strength and courage, vision and a tenacious capacity to protect what they love. And the Lord uses these men to cultivate and call forth enduring fruit through my own soul. We are made to give gifts to each other.

Finally, I write from within the throbbing heartbeat of the living church, she who is both betrothed bride and nurturing mother. May feminine responsiveness to God be quickened in her anew. For when God's infinitely creative and utterly unmerited favor bathes the waiting church, complexities give way to simplicity, fruit is born, wisdom descends among us, confidence casts out fear and the wind of the Spirit fills our waiting sails.

Simplicity

In the sixth month the angel Gabriel was sent from God to a city of Galilee named Nazareth, to a virgin betrothed to a man whose name was Joseph, of the house of David. And the virgin's name was Mary. And he came to her and said, "Greetings, O favored one, the Lord is with you!" But she was greatly troubled at the saying, and tried to discern what sort of greeting this might be. And the angel said to her, "Do not be afraid, Mary, for you have found favor with God. And behold, you will conceive in your womb and bear a son, and you shall call his name Jesus. He will be great and will be called the Son of the Most High. And the Lord God will give to him the throne of his father David, and he will reign over the house of Jacob forever, and of his kingdom there will be no end."

And Mary said to the angel, "How will this be, since I am a virgin?" And the angel answered her, "The Holy Spirit will come upon you, and the power of the Most High will overshadow you; therefore the child to be born will be called holy—the Son of God. And behold, your relative Elizabeth in her old age has also conceived a son, and this is the sixth month with her who was called barren. For nothing will be impossible with God." And Mary said, "Behold, I am the servant of the Lord; let it be to me according to your word." (Luke 1: 26-38)

"Let It Be To Me According to Your Word"

The curtain comes down on the Old Testament with the prophet Malachi declaring that Elijah will be sent to the people, followed by the coming of the Lord himself. And then...silence. Four hundred years of silence. Morning and evening, generation after generation, incensed priests lifted up the people's prayers to God. In and out of the Holy of Holies, prayers went up as hearts waited. And then one day, as though taking his next breath, God picks up the conversation as his angel Gabriel finds an astonished priest named Zechariah praying before the altar.

"Don't be afraid, Zechariah, your prayer has been heard." Here is concrete answer to earthy prayer: Zechariah's barren wife, Elizabeth, will conceive, and the child to be born will be the forerunner for the long-awaited Messiah. At this moment Reality engulfs tradition and revives revelation. There is nothing abstract about this angel or his message, and Zechariah's mind has no living categories for this vibrant creature's proclamation. And here frail faith becomes submerged in the oh-so-human desire for testable proofs: "How can I be sure of this?" Zechariah is given nine months to think it over.

Now in the sixth of these months, the angel Gabriel appears again—not this time to the communal heart of the temple, but to a humble heart in a remote village. Why

Mary? All we know is what she was told: she is "favored" by God. She is graced. God didn't go looking for a beautiful maid. He took a maid and made her beautiful.

And bathed in this terrifying, comforting favor of God, she is told of the part for which she is cast in this extraordinary drama. Mother of "the Son of the Most High." A baby born to an elderly, barren couple is a miracle with precedence; this miracle is the fruit of singular seed. If ever there was a moment to be tempted to ask for proof, it would be this one.

But our graced maid has simplicity set in her soul. And from that place she asks only for understanding. "How shall this be, since I am a virgin?" And Gabriel responds by giving her the very concrete word she needs in this moment—Nothing, Mary. God will do this great thing in you.

There are so many questions that are not answered that day. Gabriel does not tell her that the angels already have scheduled a nocturnal visit with Joseph. She does not know what will protect a pregnant teenage girl from the stones reserved for those with unspeakable secrets. Mary is given only what she needs to obey in that moment. It is all really quite simple. "I am the handmaiden of the Lord. Let it be to me according to your word."

And the simplicity of that first "yes" sets the trajectory for a lifetime filled with one grace-filled assent after another.

Favored Fullness

Simple Sparrows

My husband and I adopted a new set of offspring this year. We live in a Chicago suburb where our natural assets are the mature trees that line our lots, but over the past few years I have become aware of an odd silence in the neighborhood. Where did the birds go? I should have been waking to a cacophony of chirps and whistles that were emanating from something more alive than the drone of early morning cars beating the rush hour into the city. So we decided to entice some birds into our backyard. We bought three different kinds of feeders and filled them from bags of seeds adorned with pictures of our promised friends—yellow finches, chatty cardinals, red-winged blackbirds. The blackbirds came, with a lovelier song than I had known them to possess. But the yellow finch seed was eaten by gluttonous mourning doves, and the cardinals rarely made their presence known except as they chattered down at us from on high.

The congregation that finally adopted our backyard was composed of house sparrows. Dozens and dozens of house sparrows. They descended around and under all three feeders, and appeared blissfully ignorant of any particular seed they were supposed to prefer. Since each one of them ate the equivalent of half their body weight every day, we went through a great deal of birdseed over the summer.

Being a lover of spectacular beauty, I was, at first, rather disappointed. And then I was amused. Of course it would be sparrows. What else would God send to the Waterman home in a summer when *His Eye is on the Sparrow* was the family anthem? And then, for a single week, I was amazed. First I saw a bird swoop in, pick up a seed, and, flying straight back to her offspring, drop the seed into a hidden mouth resting somewhere in the honeysuckle bushes. This pattern was repeated for several days, and then a new phase appeared—the fledgling sparrows had now taken their place at the feeder, eager mouths open to receive whatever was offered from next door. A week later I could no longer distinguish elder from youth.

If ever there were a picture of the grace of creaturely simplicity in the Scriptures, it must surely be the sparrow. God knows them, and it never occurs to them to worry that he might forget them.[1] God feeds them and they do not fret about where their next bite will come from.[2] God even makes a home for them near to his heart, right under his altar.[3] They mate, nest, feed, mature, fly—all within the gracious provision of God's tender care for the small and insignificant.

This in-graced response of simplicity is one of the most precious gifts extended to those hidden under the gentle hand of God. Even for philosophers who ponder beauty in all her facets, simplicity swiftly rises to the surface as one of her chief attributes. "*Simplicity* refers to an essential purity, a freedom from superfluities, useless accretions and needless complications."[4] Simplicity is weightless fullness. And she is the downy foundation of all the stronger responses yet to come.

Feminine Contours

Having issued my initial disclaimer on the shy character of feminine reality, I do want to begin with a modest description of what I am talking about. In this book "feminine" includes all created things that find themselves drawn into vital connection with an outside source. This external source initiates something new to be held within, a new thing that changes the bearer even as it grows hidden within her. In the fullness of time, this new thing is brought forth anew through the bearer to take its own unique, living place in the world.

These elements form the contours of all that we know as "feminine."[5] They are found in the earth and in physical and spiritual mothers, they lie at the very foundations of the church and in the souls of every member held within her.

I encountered the elemental nature of feminine reality in creation last winter as I was writing and resting in a little cabin in the woods out in western Illinois. My love affair with birds began in this place a few years back, but for some reason they weren't coming around to my birdfeeder on this particular weekend—not even the sparrows. So I thought I'd give nature a little nudge. I took some handfuls of seed and scattered them over the snow, from tree to cabin, from path to window.

I was sitting in front of that window at dusk when five deer made their stately way up through the thicket. Three of them stopped to nibble on the low branches of the evergreen before me. But two of them kept on coming. They followed the seed. Eventually one doe followed it all the way to the window. And then she looked up and I found myself with nothing but a pane of glass between my eyes and the deep, unfathomable pools gazing back at me. Neither of us moved. I don't know what the doe received. I received the gift of utterly simple peace, and found myself blessed again with a mind and voice that was free to cry "glory."

> Of all the creatures both in sea and land
>
> Only to Man thou hast made known thy ways
>
> And put the pen alone into his hand,
>
> And made him Secretary of his praise.[6]

In the doe I again tasted our fundamental feminine posture before God, this time in an alive but inarticulate beast resting from within the depths of her creatureliness. Who would not want to be wrapped, in such a moment, in the feminine garb of a responsive and articulate voice made to worship, adore and wonder at the God who initiates and sustains such life?

Every Christian soul is, at its core, a feminine soul. We have nothing but what we receive—this is the second contour of feminine reality. As makers made in the image of the Maker, we are also initiators and creators. But never first. The raw material of our physical and spiritual life comes at the will of a divine initiative that we have done nothing to capture. We are simply favored by God. And in response perhaps we, like our sister Mary, ought to be greatly troubled at the saying and wonder what sort of greeting this might be.[7]

There is no stronger initiative than completely unmerited favor. Why did the Father not crush this broken world and start over again? His hand is certainly mighty enough to snuff us out as though we were the smoking matches my son delighted to reach for in his younger days. Why, instead, did he beget a son, born of woman, in full possession of a soul as dependently feminine as his mother's and as unwaveringly masculine as the "Most High" who begot him? This son's constant declaration,

"I can do nothing on my own"[8] is completely saturated with "I lay down my life that I may take it up again."[9]   In Jesus we glimpse receptivity so deep that no woman could taste its depths, potency so strong that no man could penetrate its power. Filled by the Father, Jesus is full. Being made full, Jesus came to fill.

If the good physician, Luke, tells us what Mary said and did, the Apostle John best engages the mystery of what Mary actually carried within her heart and womb. For what is the result of unmerited favor if it is not being made full? Fullness received, grace upon grace, word upon word. The one who leaned against our Lord's breast and heard the very heartbeat of our God understood the simple feminine fullness of a weaned child with its mother.[10] This beloved disciple knew that to be indwelt by Jesus and his Father is to be fully at home with God within our own beings.[11] Through the simple beauty of John's voice we hear Jesus bid us to abide, remain, rest.[12] Here we encounter peace that the world cannot give.[13] Here we breathe in a love that can be exhaled for others without becoming breathless. Wind that blows where it wills fills our lungs, and we are full, for that which was from the beginning came intentionally to give so that we could receive deep, lasting life. Sometimes wafting, sometimes in gales, the Holy One is always stirring up dusty earth with heaven's wholeness. Fullness initiated becomes fullness received.   The Gospel of John is dedicated to contemplating the incarnational implications of the virgin's simple "yes."

To carry such fullness changes the bearer in the very act of carrying. Part of the simplicity in this third contour of feminine reality is that so much time is spent waiting in faith for what cannot be seen or even understood. "How shall this be, since I am a virgin" is a very good question. The answer? "You *will* conceive." But Mary's conception, like our own, comes accompanied by a mystery, not a manual.

The bearer is changed as God's new thing takes root and grows in the soul that has begun to swell with the fullness of divine favor. We are not laminated channels for God's grace—aseptic containers through which his life passes without altering us in the process. While the most obvious feminine wonder is Spirit-produced fruit, the most personal wonder to be caught out of the corner of one's eye is the ever so subtle changes that occur within the bearer living as honestly as possible in the waiting. The first fleeting taste of a patience that is no longer running from pain. The secret surprise of peace filling one's breast in the midst of all that cannot be controlled. Emerging clarity in the very contexts where confusion has long won the day. Deep renewal through the simple elements of word and water, bread and wine—all of these quiet flutterings are gifts along the way, assuring us that we are the in-graced recipients of divine favor.

And finally comes the fruition of all that is feminine. Life that has rested within is to be brought forth. Everything planted in feminine soil eventually gives birth—yet miraculously, even as we have been changed in the bearing, we then give back a gift to the world that is somehow enriched for having been held awhile. God's gifts have, in their own way, become enfleshed within us. Patience that has been breathed in from heaven will be exhaled on earth, in the look in one's eye and the tone in one's voice. Sometimes that which is received is to be returned in the next moment. Pick up the phone. Write the letter. Forgive your son...and ask his forgiveness while you're at it.

But sometimes God's fullness lies hidden for a very long time. As an old friend of mine was fond of saying, "It takes a lot longer to grow an oak than a zucchini." The "fullness of time" was the result of a very long germination period.

The Apostle John's soul had carried the richness of a grace so full that the moment came when he absolutely had to exhale. And by the beginning of his first epistle, our brother is fairly bursting. He is filled with living truth, fully formed, ready to be offered the world. Perhaps we might take a deep breath and exhale with him:

> That which was from the beginning, which we have heard, which we have seen with our eyes, which we have looked upon and touched with our hands, concerning the word of life—the life was made manifest, and we have seen it and testify to you and proclaim to you the eternal life, which was with the Father and was made manifest to us—that which we have seen and heard we proclaim also to you, so that you may have fellowship with us; and indeed our fellowship is with the Father and with his Son Jesus Christ. And we are writing these things so that our joy may be complete.[14]

Whew. When the period finally appears at the end of such a lusty breath, we find what always awaits us at any birthing sired by this God. Joy. Pure, unadulterated, simple joy. If there is a secret bubbling under the feminine responsiveness at the foundation of faith, it must surely be this joy. Joy sent Mary running into the hills to find Elizabeth. Joy flies off the pen of John. Joy is what the church has sung hidden in the shadow of

God's wings,[15] or when bringing in a harvest once sown in tears.[16] Joy may certainly be more, but it is nothing less than the exquisitely simple response of a creature who is favored, the lovely fragrance of a heart that has been filled.

Nesting Birds

But as much as I love the heights from which we catch a glimpse of the favor into which we have been raised with Christ, we are always sent back to the valley. Feminine reality is blessed with a strong nesting instinct. She will not be likely to suggest setting up booths on mountains but, rather, will find her home nesting with the sparrows under the altar. If we aren't more human by the end of the day, we haven't touched her hem. There is a quiet beauty lying within the contours of our simple response as we are filled with the fullness of God. We hold the Holy Spirit's graces within and are changed by them in the very act of carrying them.

In time we offer these embodied gifts back to the world. But it's a very tangible world. I need to go fill the bird feeders. It may be God who feeds my small congregation. But apparently his means of grace at this moment is a rather short woman standing on an old stepstool who spills as much seed on the ground as she gets into the containers.

Complicated Emptiness

Pendulum Swings

One of the greatest devastations this side of Eden must be the endless internal complexities of faithlessness and fear that clutter our feminine capacity to rest. We find it so difficult to wait, like an unguarded doe or unpretentious sparrow, in order to be filled with the fullness of God. My heart aches at the brief glimpse we are given of Eden's restful communion the moment after it is no longer within reach. "I heard the sound of you in the garden, and I was afraid because I was naked, and I hid myself."[17] There is something heart-breakingly complex in the human plague of self-consciousness.

Whenever our primary focus is on self and circumstances we lose the simplicity of our connection with God. We have been made to live with hands cupped and uplifted—ready to be filled once again by the goodness of the heavenly Father who meets our "let it be" with his "here it is."

But fallen arms grow heavy and hands are more comfortably clenched. The weightlessness of simplicity is too easily exchanged for the poor substitute of finding our own fullness. We were created to be filled—humanity's miserable mystery is our insistence upon filling ourselves. We disconnect from the source of our life. We would be begetter and bearer at the same time. "I will be my own" is the barren independence at the heart of all sin. When we are caught here we function as though we live in a closed universe where no one greater than ourselves actually exists, let alone pursues us with his love.

Filled by God, our self-understanding is rooted in relationship. Who am I? One who is favored by God. But when our souls exchange this birthright for a mess of barren independence we find ourselves using our activities to define who we are. Who am I? I am what I do. Thomas Merton describes this futile definition of self in the following manner:

> The soul that projects itself entirely into activity, and seeks itself outside itself in the work of its own will is like a madman who sleeps on the sidewalk in front of his house instead of living inside where it is quiet and warm.[18]

It is hard and cold out here, and we who were made to proceed from rest are restless. Life on the sidewalk is complicated. Nothing we do out here will ever be enough. We set our eyes on what we want to attain, believing that it will fill our emptiness, only to experience hollow victory. Every independent accomplishment serves to fling us back upon our driven need to find something else to fill the void.

Sadly, this activism is not simply a fallen dynamic outside the church of Jesus Christ. She, too, can be guilty of such barren activism. It occurs whenever she tries to work for God, rather than in and through him. Not waiting to be filled she plans her programs or simply implements those that "God has blessed" somewhere else, and determines her "success" by the numbers she attracts. Her weeks are complicated and her people are exhausted. No sustained prayer, no listening obedience, no capacity simply to act on what she has received as her God leads her. When she lives from this barren place she often finds herself in competition with other local assemblies for members, and in her internal restlessness she becomes increasingly disconnected from the source of her life. When the church is caught in this activism she reaps precisely what has been sown—Christians with shallow roots whose lives are shaped by programs and methods rather than filled by the life-sustaining fullness of the Christ who is patiently waiting to embrace and fill his church and all who find their life within her.

If ever there was a complicated man, it must surely have been Peter. No resting on Jesus' breast for this one. The mere presence of a towel in Jesus' hands was enough to set his feet skittering away.[19] Peter's natural inclination was a kind of activism that was always getting him in trouble. He would get something right for a moment—"You are the Christ," and in the next breath he would be dead wrong, drawing Jesus aside to offer the kind of tempting insanity that holds up comfortable, controlled illusion as an alternative path to real life.[20]—No need to suffer, Jesus. I've got some other strategies in mind.

Between the bookends of two miraculous catches of fish we find a fisherman caught swinging at the end of his own line. Moments of clarity are consistently entangled with activistic bravado and paralyzing despair. "Lord, I am ready to go with you both to prison and to death,"[21] is the precursor to the inevitable sound of an insistently crowing rooster and a bitterly weeping man.[22]

I find in Peter's denial the same desperate hollowness I experience when my bold promises and empty activities fail to fill me with the life-sustaining grace for which I fundamentally long. In these times I am largely unaware of the deep emptiness and disillusionment that lies waiting like a mouse inside my internal crawl spaces, occasionally creeping out in my dark, unguarded moments.

For years I swung between two extremes. Sometimes I would rise in the morning, carrying on my own agenda until, disillusioned by the day's inevitable roadblocks, I would lose my way and drag my tired body to bed in defeated exhaustion. At other times I would endure longer seasons of activism and passivity. During these times I would throw myself headlong into some project—usually "for God"—and when I became exhausted I would proclaim my need for a "season of rest," which really meant nothing more than checking out of life— until I got so guilty about my stagnation that I would throw myself headlong into another project for God. I could swing back and forth in a day, a month, or a decade. Talk about dangling on the end of a fishing line.

These pendulum swings are both the source and the result of spiritual barrenness. And, when we carry our emptiness into the church, our communities of faith are susceptible to the same infection. Spiritual barrenness can spread like a virus and contaminate a whole community.

If we lose our collectively simple "yes" to God's manifold graces for life, our communities content themselves with talking about God's commandments as the poor substitute for obeying them. We do not repent of our sin, but live, instead, within unspoken agreements: "If you ignore my sin, I promise to ignore yours." We are weak and timid, and, lacking the Holy Spirit's indwelling fullness, our witness is brittle and uninviting. In these debilitating seasons the simplicity at the heart of faith is swept under the rug of soul-deadening complacency.

How are we ever to be delivered from our complicated activism, our exhausted passivity and the swing between them? We begin by recognizing the God who pursues. When Jesus finds Peter back fishing for fish instead of men, our Lord wastes no time in setting things aright. He makes breakfast, even incorporating the tangible grace of the second miraculous catch, and then, probing for all of the soul-piercing splinters, restores Peter to his first love and his true vocation.

There is no use attempting to regain our equilibrium in order to find our Savior. Like Peter, we must stop where we are, and plop ourselves down, dripping and exhausted, right at the curve of whatever complex swing we find ourselves entrapped within. When we do this, whether for the first or twentieth time, we encounter the soul-restoring favor of a God who has loved us with an everlasting love and will continue his faithfulness toward us.[23] Here there is neither striving nor shrinking. Just a quiet returning to the unmerited favor of the God whose re-creating grace is always invoking the same simple response: "I am the handmaiden of the Lord. Let it be to me according to your word."

By the time this book sees the light of day I will have lived within many simple seasons. But I will never forget the first tangibly simple season in the Waterman home. We were confronted with raw, material reality. I was leaving a place of employment and there wasn't enough money in the Waterman coffers. I had been learning to walk in the simplicity of faith for several years at that point and was rather shocked at the intensity of the unbelief that arose from my soul. I felt paralyzed and frantic all at the same time. But by God's grace I chose, like the man who brought his demon-possessed child to Jesus, to cry out, "I believe, help my unbelief!"[24] In the weeks that followed, I discovered my struggle with unbelief could be summarized in two fundamental questions: Do I really believe that you love me? And do I really believe that you are strong enough to do what you have promised? At that point the answer to both questions was, "Well, no, not really."

But I kept wrestling with these issues of foundational faith before the Lord and repented of my unbelief and the temptation to yield to both activism and passivity as they took their turns swinging through my shifting soul. I was alternatively tempted to go out to force a job to appear and to succumb to the paralyzing fear that I would never again have any gainful employment.

But over the course of several weeks, I began to know a new peace. As I deposited my last paycheck for that season I heard the Lord say, "The jar of flour shall not be spent and the jug of oil shall not be empty until the day that the Lord sends rain upon the earth."[25] A quiet confidence that we were the recipients of God's gracious favor had unobtrusively begun to calm my turbulent soul. His eye was on the sparrow in the western suburbs of Chicago. He loved us and would provide for what we needed. Since that time the Lord has provided for us through the normal means of jobs, in quiet surprises and in dramatic stories. We have never been in want. When the need has been exceptional, so has the provision.

Not long ago I was sitting on a bench in an outdoor shopping mall just before twilight. Around my feet crowded over a dozen sparrows, picking at the edges of the paving stones, tenaciously attempting to find some undiscovered crumbs in hidden cracks. I thought of the countless sparrows that now regularly inhabit my backyard, emptying three birdfeeders within a couple of days, and I wished for the language to issue an invitation to these hungry birds on their futile quest. "Come on home with me. Our Father's got more than enough for all of us."

Enemy Strikes

My peripheral vision was working well that afternoon. I caught sight of the ballistic missile long before it achieved its intended target and erupted in my face. I was on a church retreat and, at the insistence of my senior pastor, had just finished my first attempt to speak on the renewing presence of the Holy Spirit in our lives. It was, by definition, a very feminine talk, and I had spoken with fear and trembling, but also in obedience to the discernment of the leaders in my community.

Immediately afterwards this young missile sailed right into my face and hissed, "I *hate* women who teach." Having had an opportunity to brace myself during his approach I was enabled to say, "In this church we have a name for your problem. We call it misogyny.[26] And until you face this poison in your own soul you will never be whole." At that point the bomb fizzled, and I pointed him to wise men in our congregation who could help him with his need.

I do not in any way diminish the importance of thoughtful, substantive conversation on women teaching in the church. But this young man was wielding fiery darts, not the sword of the Spirit. There was no desire for truth, no commitment to love, no approach in humility in this particular encounter.

As our church walked beside this young man in the months

that followed, his underlying spiritual need became increasingly obvious: his foundational capacity to be a dependent human being in a benevolent universe was in serious jeopardy. He deeply feared relationship with God and with others. I had been the target of choice, but he was vomiting up his fearful revulsion at feminine reality herself. My young challenger's rage offered a convenient human channel for the howling hatred of the ancient enemy bent on his desperate attempt to destroy all that is creaturely and dependent.

Lucifer has always hated feminine reality—he despises all that basks in dependence on God and is thus continually being filled with a life from above. This ancient enemy's focused desire to break the primary image bearer of feminine reality has a long history. But when he succeeded in the garden, God turned his hollow victory over woman into resounding defeat. Not only was there to be enmity between woman and him, but Lucifer's nemesis would come through her.[27] Now, on this side of the incarnation, the devil's strong, independent "I will be my own" is already defeated, set in motion through a simple, dependent, feminine response: "Let it be to me according to your word."

But even as redemptive history takes its divinely appointed course this ancient enemy stalks the earth in wrath, for he knows his time is short.[28] If he can cut us off from the feminine contours at the heart of our creaturely dependence on God, what more does he need to do? He wants the creature to be destroyed. He wants little independent deities who refuse dependence at the cost of their own souls. He not only wants to make our lives barren, but to implant spiritually malignant tumors—a grotesque parody of the real thing.

He will not ultimately win. But he still bites. And while I

am not one to go looking for demons, neither will I deny the force of the demonic hatred that can come through fallen, broken human vessels who are cut off from a fundamental responsiveness to God's grace in their own souls. Broken men and women like my missile are mere pawns in the devil's schemes. After so many years now I recognize the calling card he always leaves behind. Lucifer always signs his name in paralyzing fear.

I left that retreat sobered and a bit shaken. Two days later I was carrying a glass of juice down to my son in our family room. My foot missed the bottom step and all of my weight landed on my distended ankle. As I lay writhing in pain, attempting to help my three-year old get the phone to call his dad, the thought occurred to me—this injury is not unrelated to that spiritual attack. And I was afraid.

I went through that Advent and Christmas with ice on my ankle and ice in my heart. I was frozen with fear. If this is what happens to those who ever so tentatively begin to invite others to live in feminine responsiveness to God then I wasn't so sure I was up for the ride. There was nothing simple here. Fear is complicated and paralyzing. I was numb.

Just before classes began for the winter I went on a desperate spiritual retreat. I knew that I was terrified of the mere tail of an enemy that could lash out in such inexplicable ways. I was jumping at my own shadow. My students deserved something better than a professor cowering in the corner.

But God, in his mercy, is ever the healer of our souls. And in this moment he used the very human experience of our complicated brother Peter to wrap my heart in his warmth and once again fill my soul with his goodness.

The familiar passage unrolled before my inner eye like a favorite old film. John the Baptist is dead.[29] Jesus, hearing the news, is in the process of withdrawing to a desolate place to be with his Father. But the crowds pursue him. He pauses for the day; his compassionate heart swells with healing, his benevolent hands fill with food. That night he finally draws near to the heart of his Father and sends his disciples and their boat back in the direction they came from.

But it is hard going on the water that night, and the men must have been exhausted as they look up to see an inexplicable form approaching them on the water. A ghost? No, "Take heart; it is I. Do not be afraid."

This is neither the first nor the last time that Peter will pitch himself out of a boat. It is the only time he asks for permission. "Lord, if it is you, command me to come to you on the water." "Come."

I understand this Peter. He's in me as well. "Pastor, if you really want me to teach on the Holy Spirit, I'm all there." Naïve, full-bodied risk. Leap lightly out of the boat. After all, Jesus is here. So Peter jumps out of the boat and boldly walks out to Jesus.

"But when he saw the wind, he was afraid."—Oh, wait. Maybe it isn't so simple after all. The wind is cold and lashes from every side. What am I doing here? Peter's vision gets blurred, his eyes look down at his circumstances and he begins to sink.

I sat with my ankle propped up on a pillow and my nose pressed to a window watching soft snow falling outside the simple bedroom of an old convent. There was no wind that afternoon. It was pristinely quiet. But my heart knew all about Peter's fear. Whenever the circumstances we see become all the reality we recognize, we will sink. We may sink without a fight, we may sink struggling all the way to the bottom—paralysis and frenetic activity are rooted in the same disconnected lack of focus.

But as Jesus reached out his hand to Peter, he took my own as well. "O you of little faith, why did you doubt?"—Forgive me, Lord. I have been gazing at my feet, I have been tasting hatred that hurts. Unlike Mary, I have spent these weeks feeling the sting of unflung stones. I have not gone running to the hill country to be with others who are also being filled with your grace. I have taken my eyes off you and I have not prayed "let it be to me according to your word" for many a day.

And in the next frame my icy heart completely melted. "When they got into the boat, the wind ceased."—Dear daughter, you are not called to spend your life walking on water. I give you a boat. It is filled with simple things: your family and friends, your love of nature and music, literature and laughter. Be human, daughter, and keep your chin up.—My eyes were back on Jesus and simplicity was restored to my soul. For the rest of that afternoon there was, somehow, a place made for me on that crowded boat where I, like Peter and the others, worshiped him.

From Complicated To Simple

Over the centuries the church has opened her heart and home to those who enter her through the waters of baptism. In many traditions this foundational movement from emptiness to fullness begins with an intentional journey from complicated to simple. This journey takes the form of baptismal vows.

First, the renunciations. We declare our abandonment of destructive powers in no uncertain terms. To renounce something is to say, "I will have nothing more to do with this." In baptism we renounce the enemy who wants to destroy us, the fallen powers of the world that swing us in their undulating wake, our own flesh with its natural propensity to choose deathly independence. These are the culprits that make our lives so very complicated, and as we enter the church we are bid to leave them outside. "Do you renounce Satan and all the spiritual forces of wickedness that rebel against God? Do you renounce the evil powers of this world that corrupt and destroy the creatures of God? Do you renounce all sinful desires that draw you from the love of God?"

"I renounce them."

Then, the affirmations. Emptied, we wait to be filled. Here are life-giving realities to be welcomed, embraced and held deeply within: "Do you turn to Jesus Christ and accept him as you Savior? Do you put your whole trust in his grace and love? Do you promise to follow him and obey him as your Lord?"[30]

And under the simple "I do," if we listen we may hear harmony as sweet as the song of any sparrow: "I am the handmaiden of the Lord. Let it be to me according to your word."

Receptivity

In those days Mary arose and went with haste into the hill country, to a town in Judah, and she entered the house of Zechariah and greeted Elizabeth. And when Elizabeth heard the greeting of Mary, the baby leaped in her womb. And Elizabeth was filled with the Holy Spirit, and she exclaimed with a loud cry, "Blessed are you among women, and blessed is the fruit of your womb! And why is this granted to me that the mother of my Lord should come to me? For behold, when the sound of your greeting came to my ears, the baby in my womb leaped for joy. And blessed is she who believed that there would be a fulfillment of what was spoken to her from the Lord." (Luke 1:39-45)

"Blessed is She Who Believed"

Even as the Holy Spirit overshadowed Mary she was told that her barren cousin Elizabeth was also carrying a child on whom God's blessing rested. Mary hurried to find her. She had scarcely crossed the threshold of Elizabeth's door when the gestating baby in her cousin's womb leapt at the first sound of Mary's voice. There they were: two women with wombs swelling with child, and beings filled with a joy that could only have been conferred upon them from above. Here, indeed, was "blessedness"—"the distinctive joy which comes through participation in the divine kingdom."[1]

How easy it might have been to attribute such distinctive joy exclusively to miraculous motherhood. Bystanders would do just that: years later an anonymous woman, marveling at the authoritative words on Jesus' lips, would exclaim, "Blessed is the womb that bore you and the breasts at which you nursed." And Jesus' response? "Blessed rather are those who hear the word and keep it."[2]

But from the very beginning Elizabeth understood the whole reality that Jesus would later affirm—"Blessed are you, Mary, among women and blessed is the fruit of your womb! ...And blessed is she who believed that there would be a fulfillment of what was spoken to her from the Lord."[3]

The foundation of Mary's blessedness lay in a hidden place—not in visible fruit but in invisible faith. Both Elizabeth and Jesus affirm the underlying spiritual reality that is also woven into the physical creation itself. Long before fruit can ripen, it must be implanted from a source outside itself. And in the kingdom of God, the word of God is the source that plants life-producing seed that will, in its time, bear fruit in and through the one who receives and believes.

One of the windows we have into Mary's response to the singular call placed upon her life is that she "pondered" things. She treasured up what she heard, whether from an angel, a group of ecstatic shepherds, or her own twelve-year-old son. What did she "do" with the word she received? Hers was a heart characterized by good soil, like those "who, hearing the word, hold it fast in an honest and good heart, and bear fruit with patience."[4] Gestation for Mary was more than the process of carrying a baby to term. From one angle of vision, her whole life can be understood as carrying the seed of faith to full-term—from manger to upper room, from nativity to cross to Pentecost.

Not only was there a moment in which the tree from the root of Jesse sprung up from her faithful womb. After she had nursed, nurtured and released that mighty tree there was a long, apparently dormant, season. Mary pondered and watched, treasured things up and prayed, until, one day, the life-giving Spirit of this Son filled the whole earth. And for

Mary, neither inner womb lining nor outer life experience would ever separate them again. For she, first among Jesus' disciples, was twice-blessed bearer of his life. Blessed is she who believed.

A Fruitful Life

Dust

For the first thirty-five years of my life I never gave much thought to the biblical theme of fruitfulness. It wasn't that I didn't have a vision for life. But I conceived of that vision in terms of effectiveness and success. My goals were tangible. If I worked hard enough I could be successful, and effectiveness was surely to be obtained with the acquisition of the right set of skills.

Having designed a research-driven, needs-based program for teenage mothers during my twenties, I found focus for my passion in "helping the church to be more effective." At that time, I believed that the way to accomplish this goal was to develop programs that were responsive to the felt needs of a target audience. With this goal before me, I was accepted into a doctoral program at Cornell University and spent five fascinating years earning a Ph.D. in Program Evaluation and Planning. I learned how to develop methodologies to measure program effectiveness and evaluate the needs in a community. I left Cornell at thirty-four with many tools in my kit and friends in my heart.

My path took me to Wheaton College where I joined the faculty of the Christian Education department and began my assigned task of applying my newly acquired skills to the precise goal I had initially set out to accomplish—I wanted to help the church to be more effective.

But not long into my first months at Wheaton an unfamiliar restlessness began to rumble in my soul. In retrospect I can name the source of my unrest—while I was attempting to create "effective" programs for the church with the intention of nurturing spiritual life, I wasn't really "effective" at all. People showed up. But the participants were not connecting with the Lord in any vital way. Neither was I. At the same time, my passionate undergraduates were asking their young professor what it really meant to "grow" in one's Christian life. I had all kinds of answers in my head. I had been raised in the church, taken the requisite Bible classes at my undergraduate alma mater and, out of my own spiritual hunger, done a fair amount of reading and studying Christian devotional classics. I had lots of ideas about the way spiritual growth should work. But I couldn't sustain a living connection to God through any of the means I knew. Just before my prevailing paradigm for life was completely uprooted, I was faced with the reality that I myself was lacking what was needed to be "effective" in assisting the students who were looking to me for guidance. And the devastating honesty of that realization propelled me into the terrifyingly open spaces of a far more organic faith.

Like Jane in C.S. Lewis' *That Hideous Strength*, "I was undone. Anything could happen now." And what did happen was this: my heart awakened to the love of God as he met me not only as a person, but as a woman. I wasn't offered the grace of this bracing awakening in stages—child of God, and then somewhere down the line, woman of God. God's grace blew like a storm over my disoriented, dusty heart.

My former students still remind me of the electric joy of discovery in those college classrooms during the early days when I first began to discover this new life I had been given. During that season I would cross the college quad several times a day while pondering this promise: "Lord Jesus, you are in the Father, and I am in you, and you are in me."[5] And, increasingly filled with the wonder that the Christian faith I had so long carried in my head was actually intended to fill, permeate and surround my whole being, I began to practice the Lord's presence with and within me in real life. I would drink deeply one day and invite my students to join me at the fountain the next.

There was nothing dull about those classes. I well remember the student in a large class who never spoke a word the entire semester. The room sat stunned, however, as he fulfilled a course assignment by dancing the story of temptation in Eden for us in a manner that gently but thoroughly unmasked every soul in the room. I don't remember the young man's name. I will never forget the dance.

Such classes were young and passionate, full of wonder and awe at the glory of being a soul made and re-made in the image of God. And I rejoiced with my students in the glory of discovery.

But they were also a bit wild at times. A jungle of sorts was growing up in the midst of the more carefully tended, albeit expansive, garden that characterized the college. Mixed in with the true seed of God's word in my classrooms were, no doubt, other seeds—unformed thoughts yet to be pondered well, words spoken with passion, but not always with wisdom. I, too, needed to grow, but this season of teaching ended for me—abruptly and painfully. Everything in my soul and vocation was uprooted and I was left like a plowed-up field with no choice but to wait and see what new thing would be planted there.

Yet in the midst of my aching grief rose a new, life-sustaining awareness. I was dust thrice breathed. Once God breathed, and this dust began to breathe on her own, pursuing her dusty, independent path of personal success. He breathed into me a second time, and converted barren dust to fertile soil. And, as I wandered through the newly broken-up soil of my life, I was deeply comforted by the truth that the Holy Spirit was continuing to breathe his sustaining breath into my waiting heart. And I believed.

Organic Spirituality: Christ's Life in Us

Vital Christian spirituality is profoundly organic. To be a bearer of fruit is one of the predominant scriptural indicators of ongoing maturity in the Christian life. Our souls are intended to become fertile ground in which very potent seed can take root and grow. Such seed, planted and sheltered within Jesus' church, is to be nourished by the means God chooses through the indwelling ministry of the Holy Spirit. Over time our lives are intended naturally to produce the fruit of this hidden, powerful seed planted and sustained deep within us.

The bearing of fruit is a feminine wonder. From the time she is an adolescent girl, a woman is very aware of the connection between her body's rhythms and the bearing of children. In other generations, children have actually been described as "fruit of the womb." A womb is human soil. A new life is conceived when seed is held within soil that has been prepared for it. And while this new life is to be tended well, the nature and timing of the development in an unborn child over a long gestation is outside the mother's control. No mother would ever dream of "taking credit" for the baby brought forth from her womb. That which has been knit within her is always a miracle.

Yet we can, as a contemporary culture, become detached from the greater meaning of our God-given creaturely fertility.

Without the agrarian rhythms of day and night, fall and spring, we lose our connection to seasons when the ground must lay fallow if it would bear fruit. And with the presence of artificial birth-control, we lose our awareness of the fertility cycles within our own internal seasons as well.

These creaturely feminine rhythms, however, teach us more than physical fertility. They carry foundational implications for understanding the nature of spiritual growth as well. While Christians rightly run from fertility cults who worship "mother earth," we are profoundly impoverished if an awareness of organic life does not inform our understanding of spiritual life. When it comes to Christian spirituality we are not a hydroponic people—there is no adequate substitute for soil.

Perhaps our greatest spiritual loss is the illusory assumption that we are in control of the spiritual fertility cycles within our souls and our congregations. Patrick Henry Reardon reminds us of the nature of real spiritual growth in his meditation on Psalm 1:

> The habit of prayer, this incessant meditation on God's Law, is not supposed to be something immediately useful. Trees do not bear fruit right away. They first must eat amply of the earth and drink deeply of its water. Such nourishment must serve first to build up the tree. The fruit will come later on, when it is supposed to...Some trees do not even begin to bear fruit for many years.[6]

We cannot produce spiritual fruit simply by willing it to grow. There is no forced fruit in the Kingdom of God. But, over time, the Lord can form us into the kind of people through whom spiritual fruit springs up in its season. The receptive human heart, having been quickened by the Holy Spirit, becomes fertile soil, gifted with the new capacity to receive and carry living seed that is intended, over the course of a lifetime, to bear the fruit of Jesus' life implanted in us.

Potent Seed

We cannot consider the human dimension of receptivity without first considering the primacy of God's initiating power. Our spiritual lives are barren until God implants his life-producing seed in us; this is seed that we can never manufacture or clone. And in the Scriptures, this life-producing seed is always identified as the word of God.[7]

Human words are symbols. They point to something outside themselves. Our words name things—there is the light, here the bread; they describe actions—turn on the light, eat the bread. Sometimes confused, sometimes crisp with clarity, our words are still as limited as we are.

> ...Words strain,
>
> Crack and sometimes break, under the burden,
>
> Under the tension, slip, slide, perish,
>
> Decay with imprecision, will not stay in place,
>
> Will not stay still...[8]

In contrast, when God speaks there is no disconnect between the words he utters and the reality he creates. When God uses nouns, the nouns spring into being. "Let there be light, and there was light."[9] When God pronounces verbs, the verbs leap at his command. "Stretch out your hand over the sea," and the Lord turned the sea into dry ground.[10] The word of God *is* living and active, sharper than any two-edged sword.[11] His word *does* what it says. And it is this utterly unique quality of God's word that produces its overwhelming potency.

In the fullness of time God's word took on frail flesh. As von Balthasar, pondering the incarnation, so beautifully says, "A tree planted in a flowerpot breaks it, but God can make his appearance in a creature without destroying it."[12] The voice that once "stripped the forests bare"[13] came to leave the forests intact, while causing hearts to burn instead.[14]

When this "word made flesh" spoke blessing over a few loaves of bread, the bread that proceeded from that word fed a multitude.[15] When Jesus spoke water to thirsty souls, they received a spring of living water welling up from within them.[16] When he spoke, "peace, be still," the raging waters on the lake grew calm.[17] And when he spoke his peace to troubled hearts, the same solid quiet descended.[18]

There was no false modesty in our incarnate Christ. He never shrank from the potency of the words he spoke. In fact, he consistently linked his words with eternal life itself. "The words I have spoken to you are spirit and life."[19] He did not simply point to eternal life. His words planted eternal life in human souls.

Jesus *is* what he says. And unlike the seeds we plant in our gardens, this mysterious, potent seed has no expiration date. The word-that-is-Jesus remains as capable of divine action now as when he was first given a human voice on the hills of the Holy Land.

> Once God's word makes itself heard in the world,
> in the fullness of time, its power is such that it
> reaches all men, with equal directness, and no one

suffers from being remote in time or place...It is God who is speaking, and there is no such thing as remoteness in time from his word...On the contrary, we find always the same perfect immediacy of communication that was given to those he met on the roads of Palestine: "Follow me!," "Go now and sin no more!," "Peace be with you!"[20]

When we consider the nature of this seed and its capacity to impregnate the hearts of God's people, it does, perhaps, become more understandable why human languages have consistently assigned feminine gender to the human soul. The beauty of our humanity is most fully revealed when we are most deeply receptive. We are earth implanted with life at the sound of another's words.

Receptive Soil

If we are to be fruitful, potent seed must be planted in fertile soil. Mary's response, "Let it be to me according to your word," illumines a heart that is prepared to receive the good gifts to be implanted within it. We are first wooed as we are filled with the grace that opens our hearts to the Father's love, and we are then sustained in the grace that enables us to choose to keep our hearts open to divinely imperishable seed.[21] Embedded within "blessed is she who believed" is human response to overwhelming divine favor.

Receptivity, however, must not be confused with passivity. If we are to have eyes to perceive the grace of receptivity in our lives, we must rest in the enigmatic intersection between that which God does in us and that which we do in response.

In a state of passivity we are helpless to respond—we are target, not recipient. Before the onset of our Christian lives we are, indeed, passive targets for God's grace. We are "dead in our trespasses" until God makes us alive together with Christ.[22] Dead people do not participate in the activity surrounding them—it is the ultimate state of passivity.

Having been awakened in Christ, however, we are no longer dead. The casket containing our spiritual passivity has been firmly closed behind us. Who would want to crawl back in? For when we are made alive in him, our capacity to receive from God has been called into life. The Holy Spirit now lives in us. He delights to pour the multi-faceted goodness of the Father's love upon our thirsty hearts.[23]

Receptivity's Gate

Receptivity is not passivity, but it is profoundly human. Our spiritual capacity to receive is not exotic, not something that only really "holy" people possess. Humanly speaking, receptivity is a normal activity of everyday life. Every encounter we have with each other and with the beauty of the world around us, as well as with God, opens the gate of our souls.

So come with me for a moment into the fertile land of a redeemed Christian soul. It is a vast property—once entered, we encounter a garden, and behind this well-tilled soil we glimpse meadows and hills, mountains and caves, deserts with thirst-quenching streams. We will never comprehend the soul's whole terrain in this lifetime. Having been made for eternity, the Lord's full re-creative work in redeemed souls will remain hidden to all eyes until a final trumpet announces its completion. Nevertheless, our divine Gardener delights to expand the territory of his dominion in our earthly lives—even though we have eyes that see his work but dimly.

Yet, how appropriate it is for Christian souls first to awaken in a garden. After Eden, Gethsemane and a garden tomb[24] where else would we find ourselves? The garden of our soul has a wall surrounding it, and in that wall is a strong, beautiful gate. This gate has two purposes, the first of which is to open to all that is good, beautiful and true. When our soul's gate is open we freely engage the world around us. We exchange in more than small talk over the fence with our neighbor. Rather, we invite a trusted friend, like Mary with Elizabeth, to remain awhile, to walk in each other's gardens, to treasure the miracle of the life that is growing within the other.

From inside the gate of our souls, we also gaze together upon the world outside our particular gardens. We ponder the Lord's goodness and purpose in planting within us particular expressions of his life. It often takes another's eyes to perceive and bless what God is growing in us for the good of others. And it is our part humbly to receive their blessing. For receptivity includes the willingness to be changed by what we hear. And a blessing deeply received is like water showered upon our living gardens. So it was for Mary. So it is for us.

As our souls grow, we discover that receptivity in simple moments with each other is not a different movement from the receptivity awakened by God to enable us to receive his good gifts. There is only one gate into the human soul. To be fully alive is to possess this gate in freedom, to open and close it without fear.

Of course, there is another purpose to this gate. It is intended to keep us safe from intruders who would trample the tender living things growing within as we learn to keep it shut against wolves and other predators. Here receptivity must be informed by wisdom, for we are vulnerable when our soul's gate is open. The further we open it, the more risks we take.

Sometimes we unintentionally open the gate of our souls to those who come in and trample the tender things planted there. When such bruising is accidental, we learn from the resulting pain to use discretion in opening the gate.

But forced entry is always destructive. If our inner gardens are trampled by other human beings—particularly those with some authority over us, it is far too easy for us to bolt the gate and not permit anyone access...even God.

The Lord so patiently calls us to open our soul's gate to him. When our capacity to receive has been damaged by destructive life circumstances, he carefully mends the gate so that we can, over time, begin slowly to open it before him. He does not demand that we immediately fling wide the gates of our hearts. He who does not break bruised reeds or snuff out smoldering wicks will not coerce his loved ones. But he will stand guard outside while we learn to trust him. After all, he has claimed everything within the gate as his own.

So the second purpose of this gate is to protect us, and sometime its hinges are broken and need to be mended. Sadly, that which is intended for our soul's protection can also be used for self-protection against God. It is perfectly possible to move through our lives with our gates open a mere crack to the Lord's voice. We can read the Scriptures with our ears plugged. We can mouth the words of prayers, while our hearts remain disengaged. A recurrent theme in the Scriptures is the Lord's distress at his people who go through the motions of worship with their lips, but shut the gates of their hearts against him.

It is one thing to struggle to open our gate out of fear. It is another to keep the gate locked due to our own hardness of heart. And the Lord will not normally force his way in—although he has proved himself completely capable of walking through walls.[25] Rather, just as he approached the lukewarm church of Laodicea,[26] there is a point at which he simply stands at the door and knocks. The insistent knocking itself is a gift of grace. But when we grow weary of playing in our dust pile and open the gate to admit the Gardener, we are met with forgiveness, refreshment and restoration so all-pervading that hard, dusty ground is broken up into soil that can truly sustain life.

We taste real spiritual freedom when our internal gates begin to open to receive the Lord with joy. As the psalmist cries out, "Lift up your heads, O gates! And lift them up, O ancient doors, that the King of glory may come in."[27] We tend to dwell on receptive realities most frequently at Christmas as we sing phrases like, "Oh come to my heart, Lord Jesus. There is room in my heart for thee,"[28] or, "How silently, how silently the wondrous gift is given; so God imparts to human hearts the blessings of his heaven."[29] We are not inviting our King to inhabit a closet but, rather, extending dominion to him to do what he wills with the whole estate.

And opening our soul's gate, we pray something like this, "Lord Jesus, please come in. You are so welcome here. You are the one who has made possible the transformation of our dust into fertile soil. Your Spirit dwells within. Your Father owns the land. Thank you for what is coming up that we can see. Thank you for what has been planted that we will not see for years. Truly blessed are we as we receive the grace to believe that you will plant your seed, protect its growth and bear your own beautiful fruit through our lives."

Organic Spirituality: Our Life in Christ's

When it comes to fruitfulness in the kingdom of God, the Scriptures are unapologetic about borrowing different images to invite us into this rich, multi-faceted spiritual reality. In Mark 4 alone we see Jesus using the image of a seed first as something sown in all kinds of soil and then as something that grows completely outside our awareness. In the next verse he switches his image to consider the particular case of a mustard seed. No single agrarian image tells the whole story. So, on the one hand, God's word is like seed implanted deep within us. On the other hand, we are also grafted into him as we are attached to a vine or imbedded in a tree.

The summer after I left Wheaton I was vacationing with my husband and young son up in northern Wisconsin. We drove past an orchard that had been in full bloom the year before, but this time, as we rounded a familiar corner, we were greeted by straight, bound sticks emerging from the ground. I caught my breath, and the tears began to stream down my cheeks as I stared at denuded apple trees. They had been pruned all of the way back to the trunk itself. They would not bear fruit again for years. And I knew that this was a picture of my own life as well. I had understood myself to be a fruit-bearing tree, and now I was experiencing my life as nothing more than a bound stick in the ground.

What possible purpose could there be in such brutal pruning? Why couldn't the gardener merely clip off the dead branches and shape the tree up a bit? Did he really have to turn trees full of apparent promise into barren sticks? Jesus' words became stamped on my heart: "Every branch in me that does not bear fruit he takes away, and every branch that does bear fruit he prunes, that it may bear more fruit."[30] I knew these words well. I just didn't anticipate what Jesus could possibly have meant by them.

Several years later, after apple picking in another orchard and being confronted by the distinctive shape and lush harvest of the fruit-laden trees, I went to find some botanical answers to the persistent riddle of pruning. The gardener prunes fruit trees back to where joints meet trunk so that the core of the tree might be strengthened. There are no spindly branches on such a tree. As a result of the gardener's care, the branches become thicker and stronger—more likely to stand the storms that will inevitably come upon them. In addition, pruning enables the gardener to reshape the tree so that the branches can be low to the ground and open to the sky. This image of strong branches flung wide open to receive the nutrients from above, yet formed close enough to the ground that others might pick and eat of healthy fruit, is a graphic picture of godly fruitfulness.

As I reflect back on the lush vegetation in my early classrooms and the pruning that has since occurred in more than one season of life, I have come to understand a simple truth about the challenges of learning to receive and respond to God's

unwavering favor, to live bound to our Lord in a manner that
bears fruit from within our life in Christ. The Father will take all
the time he requires to form strong disciples who are low to the
ground and open to the sky. He's a very patient gardener.

Psalm 1 offers us the richest meditation on fruitfulness, invoking
the image of the man who is like a tree. With our contemporary
translations of the Scriptures in hand, we may miss a central point.
In one such translation we read, "Happy are they who have not
walked in the counsel of the wicked..." This translation of Psalm
1 is, of course, prompted by the desire to include women in the
scriptural conversation by avoiding the language of "Blessed is the
man." But far more is at stake at this moment than gender
inclusiveness. For if we read Psalm 1 with Jesus as "the man,"[31]
the picture radically changes:

Blessed is the man

who walks not in the counsel of the wicked,

nor stands in the way of sinners,

nor sits in the seat of scoffers;

but his delight is in the law of the Lord,

and on his law he meditates day and night.

He is like a tree

planted by streams of water

that yields its fruit in its season,

and its leaf does not wither.

In all that he does, he prospers.[32]

None of us can ever claim such a life—one that never walks in the
counsel of the wicked, never stands in the way of sinners, never

sits in the seat of scoffers. There is no one who so delights in the law of the Lord that we meditate on it day and night.

There is only one man who fully bears this description. Jesus is the tree planted by streams of living water. He is the strong tree that is low to the ground and open to the sky. And he has promised us a place within his own organic life. "Whoever abides in me and I in him, he it is that bears much fruit, for apart from me you can do nothing."[33]

We become fruitful only as we receive our life within Jesus, this blessed living tree. In this tree our own frail lives rest upon root systems so deep that no enemy can dig them up, and no experience of life can shake them loose. In this tree we find ourselves protected from sweltering heat and pounding storm. Rooted in him, we become steadfast, unmoveable and well-watered. From our place within this tree we discover fruit appearing in its proper time as we are sustained by roots that draw up water with joy and a trunk that remains unbent under the weight of the ensuing crop. To be hidden in Christ is to be grafted into the very life of this strong, enduring tree that wind cannot unearth and drought cannot wither.

If, then, Christians are to be spiritually fruitful, we will simultaneously be born into His life and bear that same life within our soul's soil as we receive the potent seed of his word within our own beings. "You are in me and I am in you."[34] For our part, to be fruitful in the Kingdom of God is not primarily something we do, but the normal result of the life that has been implanted and nourished within and around us.

Our own role is that of a pregnant woman, even as we rest within the church's role as nurturing mother. Both feminine beings are to cherish the life within, to care for that emerging life to the best of our ability, to avoid anything that we know would harm the precious seed as it takes root and grows. As we, like Mary, treasure up the word of God, it has the power to shape us, to produce in us the life of Jesus.

We begin to find ourselves desiring to "bear fruit in keeping with repentance,"[35] prizing the lasting peace that roots out pervasive weeds rather than merely throwing dirt over them. Our lives become increasingly shaped by Jesus' character, producing the fruit of his Spirit in such a way that no one is more surprised than we are. Over time we become increasingly filled with fruit-bearing life in keeping with the Lord's priorities, even to the point of believing in the goodness of the Gardener when he cuts off dead branches and prunes back tangibly fruitful ones deeply attached to the vine. Blessed, indeed, is the Man…and blessed are those whose lives are rooted and grounded in him.

An Enemy Has Done This

I have two teapots resting on my desk as I write. One is a genuine *Royal Albert Old Country Roses* teapot. While it is not the finest of china, it is pretty, and this teapot is consistent with the quality of its matching pieces. The pot has a graceful shape. The china has a lovely sheen. The gold around the edges is rich and even. And the rose pattern is clean, crisp and blends into the china itself with artistic grace. The other teapot has been in my home a few weeks longer, the result of a late-night e-Bay bid. While it makes no claim to be *Royal Albert* china, the seller assured the unschooled buyer that it would coordinate with my pattern—and at a fraction of the price. The e-Bay picture resembled my teacups, and so this china rookie (and sole bidder) bought it. I was horrified when the package came and I cut through the bubble wrap to expose my new purchase. What emerged was a clunky, dull, ceramic pot with cheap imitation rose decals unimaginatively placed upon it. If I had never seen real *Royal Albert* china, I simply would have passed it by as gaudy. But sitting right next to real thing, I recognize my cheap teapot as the nauseating imitation it truly is. And I believe the same principle holds true in discerning the nature of spiritual fruitfulness. One might mistake the counterfeit for the real—until the real has been experienced. And then there is absolutely no possible comparison.

Counterfeit Seed

"In the fullness of time" God sent his Son. Jesus came to a society focused upon growing things, not one consumed with building things or replicating natural things in controlled environments. A master storyteller, our Lord drew from the natural world around him to help us comprehend the invisible kingdom he had come to bring. His agrarian parables also help us understand two dynamics that will prevent the growth of real spiritual fruitfulness in our personal and communal lives: counterfeit seed and inhospitable soil.

Jesus tells a parable in which a man sowed good seed in his field, but while he and his workers were sleeping, an enemy came and sowed weeds among the wheat.[36] When the plants came up and bore grain, the weeds came up with them. But these were no common weeds, like my dandelions, easily distinguished from the good plants around them. Instead, they were probably darnel, a weed grass "that looks very much like wheat until it is mature, when the seeds reveal a great difference."[37] Unlike the life-giving properties of wheat, darnel had little to commend it. The most it was ever used for was chicken feed—and even that was not a desirable option. This wheat-like substitute more often was thrown into the fire for fuel.

When it comes to identification of the real seed of God's word and its counterfeit, the seeds themselves might look very similar. Immature plants can be mistaken one for the other. In the discernment between wheat and weeds we must sometimes withhold judgment—until we can see the kind of fruit that is borne by each. In this particular parable Jesus was content to be patient all the way to final judgment. It is, however, one thing to acknowledge the enduring existence of counterfeit wheat sown by the evil one. It is quite another to be content to produce such counterfeit fruit.

The most confusing counterfeit to true spiritual fruitfulness in our day is a particular kind of success. When success simply means that we have accomplished what we said we would do, there is nothing incompatible with spiritual fruitfulness. Competence is not unspiritual; identifying goals and shaping life's material to meet them is a critical dimension of a fruitful life, whether in our personal contexts, our workplace or our churches.

The weedy form of success, in contrast, involves the control of more people, more money, and more power. Jesus describes such extreme hunger for this kind of success in the following manner: "Beware of false prophets, who come to you in sheep's clothing but inwardly are ravenous wolves. You will recognize them by their fruits."[38] Ravenous appetites for success can, at times, be confused with visionary passion born of good seed, whether in ourselves or in others. If the work is blessed of God, nourishing wheat will eventually be produced and those around such vision will experience both the character and priorities of Jesus in their midst. But if the work is not of God, the darnel produced will be virtually useless.

Yet we may lack the understanding to distinguish one from the other while the plant emerges from the ground. What is the essential difference between a tree that bears good fruit and bad fruit? If we cannot trust our eyes—at least for a long time—how are we to discern between the two?

To begin with, counterfeit fruit is the product of a knock-off brand of seed that operates independently of life in God. Such seed prefers to sink its independent roots in close enough proximity to be associated with real fruitfulness, while withholding the existential dependence on God that makes authentic fruitfulness possible. Any time we want to build our own kingdom and ask God to bless it, we are starting with the wrong seed. An enemy has done this.

If we truly want to be fruitful we have to give up the persistent illusion that we can both produce the seed and propagate it in ourselves. The laws of the universe will not move: we cannot be the begetter and the bearer at the same time. We can only tend seed that has been implanted by someone else. And right here we glimpse the core of the fallen human condition. We naturally prefer to be god rather than to have one. We are easily enticed by good-looking seed (or an apple) that grant us independence of movement.

I regularly experience my long-standing fallen propensity to choose an independent strain of seed to plant. I was recently charged with the task of cultivating a hospitable environment in a large church. I began, like any good academic, by reading several books that had all kinds of good ideas for fostering hospitality within the church. I struggled for months with just how such ideas might be implemented. When I finally grew quiet enough to be honest with myself, these ideas seemed sterile, disconnected, and mechanistic to me. I tentatively tried to plant a few of these seeds, but nothing would take root and grow.

And then one day, by God's grace, I realized that real, lasting hospitality could only be established in this community if the Lord would awaken love for one another in our hearts. So I began to pray the simple prayer that God would indeed quicken the love he had already planted in us, and abandoned my books and charts for coffee shops and homes. I began to make it my goal to get to know women in the congregation—leaders and followers, old members and new, young women and old. It was a clear plan, but it sprang out of real living seed that had already been planted by God's word within us. And I watched as a genuine desire to be with one another, and thus learn to love one another, began to grow in quiet ways in the life of this congregation. People spontaneously began to invite others into their homes. We had a summer Bible study where we took turns crowding into each other's outdoor and indoor living spaces. Women who had not known the person sitting in the pew next to them for the past five years were sitting down over coffee or lemonade and chatting about jobs and kids and parents—and fears and hurts and life. And real spiritual fruit began to spring forth. Jesus was walking among us, disguised in a hundred ways, yet we knew he was there through the lovely fruit that is produced in such settings—the fruit of joy. I learned a great deal about the process of real fruitfulness in that season. But the fruit only began to blossom when I ceased to rely on a sterile method and worked as though the good seed had already been planted. My job was to discern and pray, and to encourage and bless the growth of real fruit.

In order to be fruitful we must humbly receive the life-producing seed that comes from outside ourselves and set our hands to the task of caring for that which God has already planted within us. This dynamic places us in a dependent posture before God, recognizing that none of our efforts will be fruitful unless he establishes the work of our hands.[39] And so, while his good seed can be conveyed through many channels—preaching and baptizing, communion and community, great art and simple saints—it cannot be simulated. God will always be the potent source of fruit-bearing life.

If we want to be fruitful we will have to let go of our driven desire for large crowds, endless financial resources and unlimited personal power. They will never be the direct result of spiritual fruitfulness. Of course, such visible results may represent the expanding territory of God's blessing upon those who know their complete dependence on him. There certainly have been movements of genuine revival in Christian history that bear the marks of the Holy Spirit's work among us that revive people, expand resources and extend godly influence. But when our efforts are directed at people, money and power as the goal, we are nurturing counterfeit seed that, in the end, will produce chicken feed at best, and more likely, weeds simply fit for the fire.

The possibility of an insatiable hunger for more tangible results is a serious issue that ought to make us tremble before the living God. Our hearts are more naturally prone to self-deception than clear perception. We are in danger of sowing counterfeit seed whenever we place our reliance in the latest method. There is nothing inherently fruitful in materials that may, indeed, have been the instruments through which God produced real fruit somewhere else. My hospitality books were good servants but poor masters. To put one's faith in a method is to descend into a kind of magic, where we think we can control the results of living things by uttering the right incantations. If we rely on a method for success, even if we do all the steps right, the result may well be counterfeit fruit. Fruitfulness is always grounded in an existential dependence on God to plant, grow and bless. If he will not give his glory to another, why would he infuse that glory in a mere method?

Inhospitable Soil

About five years ago Wyatt and I retired an old playhouse and rusty swing set that had more than fulfilled their intended function during the first decade of my son's life. We hired a landscape designer to produce a master plan for our large, barren backyard. He conceived a beautiful stone patio that was far too elaborate for us to attempt on our own. So we had the professionals build the patio, and then Wyatt and I took up gardening. With no experience, a good plan and a lot of "sweat equity," we are gradually turning an ugly space into a peaceful haven.

But we have made plenty of mistakes over the years. And most of them have revolved around the planting of rose bushes. We haven't attempted to cultivate the finicky roses, but instead the low-maintenance ones that anyone is supposed to be able to grow. But ours kept dying. We were puzzled. We were following the designer's plan. We purchased healthy plants suited to our climate, they got the requisite amount of sunlight every day, and we regularly watered and fertilized them. But after losing two rounds of rose bushes that were supposed to be surrounding our seat wall on the patio, we pulled out the desiccated roots and decided to dig deeper. What we soon discovered was a mountain of sand. The patio professionals had finished their work, covered over the excess sand with enough dirt to hide its presence and gone their way. And we hopefully planted our roses each year, and each year watched them die. Once we removed the sand and filled it all in with the good dirt, manure and peat moss recommended for roses, our bushes took on a whole new life.

It matters that good seed is planted in the soil. But if the soil cannot properly receive it, the seed will not bear its anticipated fruit. I have wondered if the parable of the sower[40] might not have been more aptly entitled the parable of the soil. The sower doesn't change. Neither does the seed. It is the relative receptivity of the soil that changes. And, while we are helpless to plant the good seed in our souls, we who have been made alive in Christ are not completely helpless in facing the state of the soil in our hearts. In every human heart there are rocks and thorns that need to be dealt with as our hearts are being made increasingly fertile earth for the seed of God's word.

Rocks

When we consider rocky soil, the text in the Gospel of Luke reads this way:

> The ones on the rock are those who, when they hear the word, receive it with joy. But these have no root; they believe for a while, and in time of testing fall away.[41]

The only action in the Christian life that breaks up rocky soil is repentance. As the prophet Jeremiah cried out, "Break up your fallow ground, and sow not among thorns."[42] The capacity to repent is itself a grace of God, but one that must be received with an open heart. As Psalm 139 concludes,

> Search me, O God, and know my heart!
>
> Try me and know my thoughts!
>
> See if there be any grievous way in me,
>
> and lead me in the way everlasting![43]

Our hearts are like fields with superficial rocks all over them and subterranean rock shelves deep within them.

This reality is troublesome to some Christians who want to believe that, when we confess and are forgiven of our sins, all the rocks go away as well. But they just keep surfacing. So either we conclude we haven't confessed enough, which will send us down a road of morbid introspection, or else some other dynamic is in play here. When we confess the sin of which we are aware, the Lord promises to forgive it all. "He is faithful and just to forgive our sin and cleanse us from *all* unrighteousness."[44] Communion to God is restored. The good seed is renewed within us.

But Jesus did not come only to reconcile the world, "not counting our sin against us," but to recreate the world and make of us a new creation. [45] And so, while our sins are forgiven as the pebbles and rocks we readily confess surface and are removed, the

Lord is in the business of expanding the territory in our hearts. He "enlarges the place of our tent"[46] over time by showing us new rocks that have been hidden under the surface—rocks that he let lie until the right time for them to be revealed and carried away.

Because of the Father's love that hates everything that destroys the creatures of God, the Holy Spirit continues to reveal the rocks that lie just under the surface—anger when I am not given whatever I believe is due me, my quick propensity to judge rather than show mercy. Not long ago I was deeply convicted of a newly protruding rock while reading the great seventeenth-century poet, George Herbert. In *The Church Porch* he poses the question, "Why should I feel another man's mistakes more than his sickness or poverty?"[47] Why, indeed? Another rock exposed that it may be removed.

One could ask why God permits rocks to lie buried for so long and then is so insistent upon making them visible. This is one dimension of his mercy—if I were to see all of the rocks lying underneath the topsoil of my life at once, I would be driven to despair. As the Christian philosopher Dallas Willard observes:

> The possibility of denial and self-deception is something God has made accessible to us, in part to protect us until we begin to seek him. Like the face of the mythical Medusa, our true condition from God would turn us to stone if we ever fully confronted it. It would drive us mad. He has to help us come to terms with it in ways that will not destroy us outright.[48]

The Lord is gracious and full of compassion—and knows what we can handle. To my mind, one particular moment of spiritual genius in the traditional Lutheran confession is this phrase: "I, a poor miserable sinner, confess to you everything I have ever done..." When I first began to pray this prayer I was quite puzzled. Not only was there not time for such a recital, but hadn't God already forgotten those things? However, over time I have begun to understand. A rock that is newly visible to me has been there all along. The Lutheran confession gives the people of God the language to confess newly uncovered rocks...in the Lord's time.

But while clearing the fields of the rocks just under the surface represents one level of our sinfulness, there is another kind of rock that is present in the deceitful human heart. We do not consist of topsoil alone. There are layers of rock deep in the substrata of our beings. We cannot search for them. When the Lord wants to reveal pervasive, underlying sin within us, he will orchestrate the events to bring the buried layers into the light. Relentless in his love, he is also a gracious healer and he will not leave us without resources when it is time for these imbedded layers of rock to be revealed.

One late spring I came face to face with one such substratum of pervasive rock. I was having lunch with one of my colleagues from Wheaton College on a Friday afternoon. We were two tired professors at the end of a semester. Our waiter happened to be an exhausted college student. He could not pour water into glasses. He could not take the simplest food order. He was asleep on his feet. Unfortunately, this encounter was a collision waiting to happen. I really did not want to engage another sleep-deprived student, especially during a personal lunch on a Friday. As he shuffled through the meal, I became colder and colder, for when frustrated, I do not tend to erupt, but rather to send out a blast of freezing disapproval that withers incompetence on contact.

Later that evening I was preparing for class the following week, reading through Lewis' essay, "The Weight of Glory." I came to this section:

> It is a serious thing to live in a society of possible gods and goddesses, to remember that the dullest and most uninteresting person you can talk to may one day be a creature which, if you saw it now, you would be strongly tempted to worship, or else a horror and a corruption such as you now meet, if at all, only in a nightmare. All day long we are, in some degree, helping each other to one or other of these destinations...[49]

And an almost audible voice descended from heaven saying, "So Carla, what destination did you help that young man toward today?" It was a two-edged question that did not merely pierce through a moment, but sliced through an entire way of being. The Lord struck deep, pervasive rock. I was suddenly faced with the terrible truth that I divided the world into two categories of people: those whom I treated with the dignity and respect due a human being and those whom I viewed merely as a means to an end. I repented with all of my heart. I received the forgiveness of the Lord, along with the clear fruit of repentance—I possessed both a deep determination to change the way I interacted with others and an equally deep understanding that the possibility of change lay not in my own good intentions, but only as I learned to interact with others out of the life of Christ living in me.

In the days and weeks to come I began to experience an astonishing renewal. I would walk into a store or a restaurant, and life became an adventure of how my interactions might bless my newly discovered friends. I would pray that Christ would be in my eyes, in my smile, in the way I spoke, especially when the momentary circumstances were not going smoothly. Painfully aware of my own weakness, knowing that at any moment I could interact out of my old, frosty patterns—I learned to lean more fully into the Jesus who was pressing his life into me. Over time, I found consideration and patience beginning to grow in a place where only selfishness had reigned. And in the disarmed faces looking back at me from behind the counter, across the aisle and inside the uniform, I discovered a new conduit of joy.

I have in no way ascended to a higher spiritual plane in this matter. On any given day I discover remnants of the old rock protruding from my heart, and I have no doubt that its old, sharp edges scrape over some of my interactions with others. But the definitive shattering of that subterranean shelf of rock occurred over a decade ago. And I had an experience last spring that encouraged me as I realized how much my heart had truly been changed. I was standing outside the Department of Motor Vehicles early on a cold April morning. It was my son's sixteenth birthday, and we were there to obtain his driver's license. Ethan and I began our usual banter—somehow it is always my fault that he is inadequately dressed for the weather. As we were playing our typical game of verbal ping-pong, I began to hear the person behind me chuckle. After a few minutes I turned to include our neighbor in this conversation. I found myself looking into the eyes of a person that I could not identify as man or woman. I was instantly overwhelmed with Jesus' love for my new friend and we swapped stories and laughed about the relationships of adult children with their mothers until the DMV finally opened. As I commented to my son later, "For just a moment we are enabled to give a lonely person the gift of 'normal.'" When Ethan and I had finished our business, I looked around to see my friend's eyes glued on us, and I smiled, waved good-bye, and suddenly remembered the tired waiter so many years before. There is nothing theoretical about real spiritual transformation. Jesus is perfectly capable of breaking through the deep rocks in our souls so that he can saturate us with his love for the world. We have only to repent of what we are shown and follow him out of our heart's confining quarry.

Thorns

But on the other side of the rocky soil broken up by God's forgiving, expansive grace and our repentant response, we find one more kind of soil that needs attention if we would possess receptive hearts able to bear the good seed of God's word to fruition.

> As for what fell among the thorns, they are those who hear, but as they go on their way they are choked by the cares and riches and pleasures of life, and their fruit does not mature.[50]

Just as counterfeit seed is, in our time, produced by a particular version of success, so these thorns take on the form of a particular kind of distraction. The sheer amount of activity in our lives is, in fact, our culture's most popular definition of what makes a life worth living—and, simultaneously, our chief source of complaint about those lives. The tourist industry thrives on the myth that "getting away from it all" can be achieved by physically removing oneself to an idyllic location for a week or two. But it's a lie. One can be sunning on a tropical beach with a distracted heart. And one can move through a full, normal day with a quiet heart.

External quiet does not guarantee internal quiet, and external noise does not preclude internal solitude. I doubt Mary's circumstances were idyllic in a jam-packed village with shepherds, sheep and whoever else followed behind as they pressed in close to her and her child. Neither do I think her external or internal circumstances were conducive to quiet after three days of looking for her twelve-year-old man-child in Jerusalem. But these are the two passages in which we are told that she "treasured up" these things in her heart.[51] Through the long months of her waiting and being tested by circumstances beyond her control, Mary's quiet, receptive heart had been strengthened in the midst of cares that could easily have choked out the faith growing deeply within her. I do not find it surprising that, in this same gospel, Jesus describes the good seed planted in good soil in a manner resembling his mother's heart:

> As for that in the good soil, they are those who,
> hearing the word, hold it fast in an honest and
> good heart, and bear fruit with patience.[52]

We do not face the upheaval of a Roman census, the inability to make prior reservations at the inn or the absence of well-networked means for swiftly attempting to locate missing sons. But each generation has its own challenges when it comes to facing the "cares, riches and pleasures of life" that prevent the maturation of spiritual fruit.

Perhaps the enemy's greatest playground at this point in history is his attempt to sever us from the fundamental limitations of our humanity. We only have twenty-four hours in a day and we can only be in one place at a time. And we live as though these limitations do not exist. But they will not go away. The human limitations of time and space constitute a law of the universe, and they will not go away because we are running too fast to acknowledge them.

Early in my discovery of a receptive life before God, I began to confront my unwillingness to face these two unwavering human limitations. I had more work to do than could physically be accomplished in any given span of time, and I frequently found myself feeling guilty about being in one place when I suspected I should be somewhere else. I sincerely desired to reorder my over-committed life but had no idea where to begin. As I asked the Lord for understanding I received a picture that has been of great assistance to me ever since.

I saw my life as a tangled mess of ropes, each one representing some commitment I was carrying at that point in my life. And I had no idea how to untangle them. In my prayer I held them up to Jesus and said, "Here. I'm exhausted and overcommitted. I have no idea how to get this mess in order. Will you help me?" Over the next few months my heart repeatedly returned to this prayer and its accompanying picture, and, over time, I saw the Lord take the whole mess and untangle the ropes. Some of them he set aside and said, "I never intended for you to carry these ropes. That was your idea." I confronted all of the presumptuous commitments I had taken on because they would be "a good experience" which, being translated, meant that they were calculated to look good on a resumé. Other ropes looked frayed and were gently laid in another pile. I seemed to hear the Lord say, "These once belonged to you, but not now. If you hold onto them, you will block others from stepping into the places I have for them." I faced all of the school and church commitments I had taken on—either because I thought they would fall apart without me or because no one else was apparently there to pick them up. One by one, as each commitment came to their natural conclusion at the end of a year or a term, I let them go. In several cases others with more vision and more appropriate gifts stepped forward to fill the vacant places. The ropes began to thin out. "Here are the legitimate ropes that are yours to hold." They were solid and permanent: family, church, vocation. I found myself breathing deeply and without panic for the first time in a long while. And then I began to realize with some astonishment that as the tangled ropes were gradually sorted out, the Lord's fists were getting rather empty. After several months he introduced a couple of new ropes. "Here, you have room for these now. I want you to carry this new rope in this season." For the first time in my life I had room to discern the best from the merely good. Finally the picture revealed one last frame. I saw the Lord gather all the legitimate ropes of my life in his hands. Then he said, "Daughter, I will hold the ropes, and hand you the one that you are to carry in this day, in this place. Look to me and I will guide you."

I have now lived well over a decade since that fundamental season of reordering. Many of the years have been exceedingly full, but rarely frenetic. A few have been very quiet, but never empty. We are all invited to taste the internal composure that is the legacy of those who would join Mary as she refuses to be choked by the cares of life, but rather, ponders what she has seen and heard. Like a pregnant woman attending to the child in her womb, ever aware of its expanding life, we are to learn to hold steady, with our hearts lifted to the Lord, waiting for all the good fruit that is yet to come. "Blessed, indeed, is she who believed that there would be a fulfillment of what was spoken to her from the Lord."

Wisdom

"My soul magnifies the Lord,

and my spirit rejoices in God my Savior,

for he has looked on the humble estate of his servant.

For behold, from now on all generations will call me blessed;

for he who is mighty has done great things for me,

and holy is his name.

And his mercy is for those who fear him

from generation to generation.

He has shown strength with his arm;

he has scattered the proud in the thoughts of their hearts;

he has brought down the mighty from their thrones

and exalted those of humble estate;

he has filled the hungry with good things,

and the rich he has sent away empty.

He has helped his servant Israel,

in remembrance of his mercy,

as he spoke to our fathers,

to Abraham and to his offspring forever."

(Luke 1:46b-55)

"My Soul Magnifies the Lord"

There is no doubt that Mary spoke most eloquently through the silent gestation of the baby being formed within her womb, yet she also received profound words of wisdom that quickly took root in her heart. While her womb was the recipient of the Most High's only begotten seed, her mouth was the bearer of the Most High's intentions toward his people, and this young girl did not hesitate to give voice to her understanding of God's redemptive design in the presence of her trusted relative, Elizabeth. Her song, the "Magnificat," is an exquisite recital of the Lord God's mighty deeds throughout the history of Israel.

Mary begins by telling of her own encounter with God and its amazing implications for the generations to come, but she does not dwell there. She swiftly lifts her gaze to all men and women of humble estate who, like her, are raised up by the mercy of this mighty God. She proclaims God's strong arm in caring for the humble and hungry and thwarting the plans of those who rely on their own resources to carry them through. But this is no abstract truth, assented to with Mary's mind while her heart remains a stranger to its warmth and depth. She who proclaims this great reversal remains completely at rest in her own "humble estate." Throughout it all she can only marvel at the might and mercy of Israel's God.

Little voice. Great song. And in her deep sensitivity to the Spirit of God she received divine insight brought forth so clearly and joyfully that, looking back, the church has seldom been content to leave these words unaccompanied. Mary's "Magnificat" has, more often than not, been sung.

And no one sang her song more fully and deeply than her son. Mary's well-digested wisdom of the Father's priorities of humility, mercy and care for the poor was as firmly implanted in Jesus' heart as her milk was inextricably bound into his flesh and bones.[1] Even as Mary recognized her own humble estate, her son would identify himself as "gentle and humble in heart" and call for the same humility to be made manifest in his servants. As Mary recounted the Lord's tremendous mercy to those who fear him, Jesus would put flesh to his Father's character by healing the beggars and blind men who cried out to him, "Lord, have mercy." He would teach his followers to be merciful and challenge the mercilessness of his critics. And, even as Mary proclaimed the Lord's heart for the poor, Jesus began his own ministry by proclaiming that he had come to preach good news to those whose hands and hearts were waiting to be filled. What her soul had magnified, her son's soul now multiplied. The Mighty One had, indeed, done great things.

Wisdom from Above

How Shall We Live?

As a Christian doctoral student with the goal of "helping the church to be more effective," my graduate work at Cornell University included an emphasis on the interface between public law and Christian faith. I had not recognized Cornell's unique ethos before I arrived there, but because it is the only Ivy League university that prides itself on being established on a "non-sectarian" foundation, the culture itself made for some very interesting challenges once I came.

One of the most memorable of those challenges came through a connection I formed with a young ethicist who taught a course on "Public and Private Morality." Here the cultivation of personal moral virtue was essentially irrelevant in public contexts. Whether a leader was motivated by pride or humility had no place in the conversation. The only personal moral quality I recall discussing in class was neutrality.

Rather, a more formulaic "calculus" supplanted personal virtue, particularly when moral decisions involved large groups of people. What decision would create "the greatest happiness for the greatest numbers?" If some people needed to be discounted in the decision, who should they be and on what basis? Here the foundation of all action, while manifest in several different forms, was always a humanly devised rationale or set of rules.

I felt as though I had landed on an uninhabitable planet. There were moments where I could scarcely breathe and certainly hours where I could not find ground on which to stand. I was utterly in over my head. But I was an undaunted fumbler and I would offer inadequate, albeit impassioned, attempts to articulate why this approach seemed so fundamentally wrong to me. I was the token, inept defender of a deep Christian tradition that I intuitively knew to be true, but lacked the understanding to articulate. Nevertheless, the professor, if not my fellow students, always responded to my unformed ideas with a respect for me as a person that displayed more personal engagement than the equations he was espousing.

So while this professor stood on the opposite shore from where I was firmly, if not lucidly, planted, we formed a kind of friendship—forged out of a shared respect for personal conviction and a mutual commitment to the original meaning of toleration, which sought to understand opposing views not because the issues did not matter, but precisely because they mattered so much. After the course concluded I continued to work with him on related topics, and toward the end of this season I found myself in his office drinking espresso and talking about the various ideas on the table. At one point I looked at him and said, "You know, in all of the reading and wrestling with these moral issues, I am grateful for all the terrain you have helped me explore, but I want you to know that my fundamental convictions have not moved an inch." He set down his cup, swore, gazed at the wall with wry amusement, and then this wandering son of an Anglican priest looked me in the eye and said, "Carla, the significant difference between you and me is that you have a connection to God, and I do not."

I was astounded by his honesty, even as I ached for this brilliant young professor. If, as he assumed, he really was alone in the universe, then a reliance on moral formulae of various sorts was at least an honest attempt at navigating his steps through a world where he encountered no one wiser than himself.

A few years later I was on the other side of the podium. And, while not teaching ethics, I was teaching a human development course where the question, "how shall we live?" inevitably crept in. So, by way of introducing a conversation on wisdom, I played a game with my students. I would read the following set of character qualities and then ask the men and women in my class to identify the biblical source. "Meek, pure, peaceable, gentle, open to reason, full of mercy, full of good fruits, impartial, and sincere."[2] In at least half of these classes, always filled with very bright students, the response would come, "Oh, that's the Proverbs 31 woman." Oh, well, actually no. They are characteristics of the wisdom from above found in James 3.

But my students were not far off. These attributes are also completely consistent with the feminine personification of wisdom in the book of Proverbs. Here wisdom is painted as a mother calling to her children in the streets,[3] as a wife more precious than jewels,[4] as a sister who walks beside and speaks truth to us,[5] and as a hostess at a nourishing banquet.[6] Perhaps we are not as isolated as my ethics professor believed us to be.

In Wisdom's House

Christian wisdom dwells among us whenever God's grace and truth are accessibly communicated to ordinary people in real time. Wisdom is not lofty, although she is deep; she is not unobtainable, and, once possessed, she quietly instructs. When Mary sings the *Magnificat*, she not only bursts forth in praise, but she walks out of the Old Covenant and into the New, carrying with her the essential riches of God's self-revelation to Israel.[7] God is mighty. His mercy endures forever. He establishes the humble and dashes the plans of the proud. Mary places these inherited jewels of wisdom on deposit in this song, in expectation of the day when God's eternal priorities will again be revealed in all that is becoming new.

Mary embodies a wisdom that has long been personified in feminine form. Perhaps the most illuminating moment in the long scriptural tradition of the feminine embodiment of wisdom appears in Proverbs 9. In this context she is named "Lady Wisdom." To approach her house is to encounter a queenly humility that has much to teach us about the jeweled qualities of wisdom received from God.

> Wisdom has built her house;
> she has hewn her seven pillars.
> She has slaughtered her beasts;
> she has mixed her wine;
> she has also set her table.
> She has sent out her young women to call
> from the highest places in the town,
> "Whoever is simple, let him turn in here!"
> To him who lacks sense she says,
> "Come, eat of my bread
> and drink of the wine I have mixed.
> Leave your simple ways and live,
> and walk in the way of insight."[8]

When we first glimpse Lady Wisdom she is carefully laying the scaffolding for her home, preparing a nourishing meal and setting a welcoming table. There is both creativity and intentionality in wisdom's work. She's not in a hurry. Building a house—particularly one with eternally significant pillars[9]—is not the spiritual counterpart to pre-fabricated housing. There is much to be done before anyone is invited to the banquet. But such preparation is not onerous. One does not sense any striving here; only the intentional joy of foundations well laid and a meal creatively planned and lovingly prepared.

Wisdom's Creativity

One of Lady Wisdom's best secrets is how creative she really is intended to be. Becoming wise is an adventure. The journey begins when, as the Apostle Peter exhorted new believers, we take in "pure, spiritual milk"[10] offered by wise counselors around us. But we truly discover of the joy of wisdom's creative adventure when, in the language of the Apostle Paul, we ourselves learn to eat solid meat as we inwardly digest God's nourishing word for ourselves.[11]

There comes a point in the Christian life when we ourselves are intended to "build our house and set the table." As we draw in deep spiritual sustenance from above, real spiritual creativity is birthed from within us. We begin to offer what we have digested in a form that can appropriately be received by others. In so doing, those around us are given the opportunity to share in a meal of real spiritual nourishment.

Having come to appreciate this creative dimension of wisdom, I take great delight in observing this divinely inspired creativity taking shape for the benefit of others. My sister, Pam, in addition to drawing the illustrations for this book, has other, more hidden, talents. Her alter-ego is a red-headed muppet-like puppet called "Max" who, for a season, was the favored celebrity among the children in her church community. Over the course of a year Pam and Max taught the Lord's Prayer to young children—clause by clause. She had been reading classic theological works on this prayer and pondering the implications for her own life. She then translated the truth she had received into a form children could hear through a loud, dramatic puppet. When they reached, "as we forgive those who sin against us," Max sat writhing in pain on her lap as he told her of a friend who had lied about him on the school bus. Max wanted to smash his face in. Instead, Pam assisted Max to let go of his desire to pummel his friend and let Jesus deal with this boy's hurtful behavior by taking a helium balloon, drawing a representation of the lying friend's face on it, and then releasing the balloon. Max and the children watched as the balloon rose to the top of the rafters, and they all received a simple image of what letting go of vengeance actually might look like.

One of the greatest joys of growing in godly wisdom is that, as she establishes her presence in us, wisdom becomes a permanent resident in our souls. This facet of God's grace can be shared in innumerable contexts by richly creative means, without any loss of it within ourselves. In fact, the very act of sharing wisdom only seems to strengthen our understanding. I don't know of anything more fulfilling than being able, like the scribe, to bring forth wisdom's treasures, whether old or new,[12] in a form that can be received by others—even through a red-headed puppet named Max.

Wisdom's Spirit

While Lady Wisdom's preparation is marked by substantive creativity, she has no need to draw attention to herself. "Look at me!" could not have been further from her mind. When it comes time to offer her gift to others, she quietly attends to her own meaningful activity and sends her young women out to issue the invitation. Evidently, she has passed on what she knows to such a degree that she trusts the younger ones to issue as winsome an invitation as she herself would have offered. The point is the invitation to the meal, not the inviter.

It is one thing, however, to recognize humility as a primary distinguishing mark of godly wisdom. It is a very different matter to appreciate the taste of such humility in real time.

While I was on Wheaton's faculty I was once invited to address a sub-committee of college trustees concerned with the spiritual life of students on campus. By this time I was learning to open the gate of my heart to the Lord and, after so many years of living confidently at ease in my own independent resources, I was trying to learn how to receive wisdom for actual contexts. After considerable thought and prayer, I believed that I had what was required for this presentation.

We took turns giving our reports—one page, bullet-pointed executive summaries with a few minutes of relatively engaged discussion on each report. About half-way around the room they came to me. I had no written report. I just had a verbal picture. "The students who come to us are all wearing old coats of some sort—coats that hide their sin and woundedness inside. And my job as a spiritual formation professor is to help them take off those old coats and receive the new clothes the Lord would put on them." There was a long pause. After what seemed to me to be an endless silence, the next person began their bullet-pointed report. However, for the rest of the meeting the image of "old coats" kept emerging in the conversation.

Looking back, I realize that the simple picture of "old coats" was immediately useful because it was wise. It was a word spoken in season that assisted the group to perceive more concretely and deeply the spiritual reality we were talking about. But at the time I felt awkward and embarrassed. No one had engaged *me*. I had not yet learned that genuine wisdom received from God is not self-referential. The wisdom is in the word, not in the recognition of the bearer of the word. I walked many years before I began to rejoice when a word aptly spoken could be the means by which God's good seed took root and grew in others—regardless of whether the messenger was ever recognized or not.

Lady Wisdom's invitation as humbly conveyed through her young women does not disappoint. In her house is found correction—"reprove a wise man and he will love you;"[13] nourishment—"come, eat of my bread and drink of the wine I have mixed;"[14] guidance for the road ahead—"leave your simple ways and live, and walk in the ways of insight;"[15] and the encouragement to walk that road to its end—"For by [wisdom] your days will be multiplied, and years added to your life."[16]

I wonder if Elizabeth was not Mary's "Lady Wisdom" in human form. The angel Gabriel did not reveal a great deal to Mary, but he did give her information that was received as practical guidance. Mary hurried to the one home in the hill country where the silent miracle she carried would be understood. As Elizabeth welcomed her, wisdom was kindled in this older cousin, and the Holy Spirit filled her lips as well as the womb where John lay resting within. In Elizabeth's house, Mary received one blessing after another. Not surprisingly, it was here, in the safety of this nourishing home, that Mary was enabled to give voice to the deep insights welling up from within her heart even as "the wisdom from on high"[17] took possession of her womb.

Wisdom's Ways

Between "Lady Wisdom," Elizabeth and Mary, we begin to glimpse the treasure we are intended to receive, hold, be changed by, and give back to the world. For in the midst of life's challenges and trials there is unspeakable joy awaiting us as we come to know ourselves to be creatures dependent upon a loving God and learn to look up and receive concrete guidance for our lives. We find the Lord resting in every corner. The wisdom received is solid and creative, and produces in us that which is patient, humble and nourishing. Those who taste of this fruit are sustained and can be encouraged to walk with us in the way of insight.

Godly wisdom does not, however, live in the stratosphere, in rarified air that only a few particularly spiritual people can breathe. To grow in wisdom we must live low to the ground and present to the daily-ness of life. The need to ask for wisdom from above arises from real life contexts.

A friend and I explored this theme on my patio one day. She was in town for a brief visit and we sat drinking tea and catching up with life. She had just moved to a new situation, away from familiar work, beautiful spaces and valued friends, and she was experiencing the exhausting emptiness of a job that was too complicated, a context where she felt undervalued and a place where friends were not naturally found. The tears filled her eyes as she spoke of her weariness, her disillusionment and her anger. My friend is a fighter—she wants to right wrongs for herself and others and she wants to demand a human pace and human respect. She wants to know and be known. But she was finding herself weak and struggling instead. And as I listened, I realized that she was doing everything she knew to navigate a very difficult situation.

After listening to her pour out her heart over the first cup of tea, I offered her a second, along with this provocative observation from Dorothy Sayers' *The Mind of the Maker.* "Life is not a problem to be solved, but a medium for creation."[18] And I suggested, "Perhaps it is time to drop your sword and pick up your paint brush."

And so we were off…exploring the internal battles that we so often fight with others even when they never actually experience the swordplay in our souls. We spoke of the weariness created by internal turmoil and that lack of quiet within ourselves that adds to the general frenetic emptiness. And then we turned to the pallet of colors she had been given in this season—not the rich reds, golds and blues that this friend would naturally reach for, but a more subdued set of tones…grays, browns with few shades of tan to add some interest. Could there be beauty in this season? Could life be a medium for creation…even here? As we talked I found my heart pondering this fundamental truth: when there are so many things over which we have no control, we still have the choice of whether to wield a sword or pick up a paintbrush.

This clear image of creativity in the midst of our very earthy trials has stayed with me over the months since my conversation with this friend. I have found myself, more than once, specifically asking for a kind of poetic wisdom from above, a wisdom that can bring beauty into the messiness of chaos, and peace into the midst of pain. God continues to be faithful. He delights to give good gifts to his children. And I am learning to pray these prayers with growing confidence. For so many years I put creativity in one corner of my life and discernment for life's trials in another. But somewhere along the way I began to discover that they are not separate. Wisdom is intended to be beautiful.

The Source of Wisdom

Nothing is more beautiful than wisdom's source. The incarnation of our Lord Jesus Christ is a many-faceted jewel to be pondered with wonder for our whole lives—and then, I think, we will start all over again when we gaze into the intimately familiar, yet unimaginably radiant, face of our ascended Lord. And one of the facets of this jewel is that this second person of the Trinity was at the Father's side at creation.[19] The wisdom of God was a "master workman" rejoicing in the Father's inhabited world. Yet this same second person of the Trinity became a child who "grew and became strong, filled with wisdom."[20] After his adventure in the temple at twelve, we are told "Jesus increased in wisdom and in stature and in favor with God and man."[21] By the time the world was awakening to Jesus' presence in the world, people were marveling at the kind of practical wisdom that could even rule the wind and the sea.[22] Who was this man?

One of the mysteries of the incarnation is that Jesus was not only completely open to being filled with his Father's wisdom, but actually required such filling. Why would he who was at the

Father's side at creation need to filled? Didn't he come to us full, like a divine pre-paid phone card that had only to be used up?

But divine wisdom was now carried in a human frame and lived within a human mind and heart. Jesus himself was continually being filled with wisdom from above and carried his insight and understanding in a mind and heart just like ours...except that there were no dark corners in him—every physical and spiritual atom in his being was filled with light. And then, on the other side of his willing existential knowledge of our ignorance, weakness, brokenness, sinfulness and rebellion, Jesus is revealed after his ascension to be the Lamb who was slain and "is worthy to receive power and wealth and wisdom and might and honor and glory and blessing."[23] All the treasures of wisdom and knowledge now reside in the one who first took on our mind that he might give us his own.

Here we glimpse godly wisdom's lovely dance. The Father filled his incarnate Son with the wisdom needed to navigate unparalleled challenges on this earth. As we read the Gospels we are reminded of the astonishingly creative wisdom granted to Jesus in the most challenging venues of his earthly life—his silence in the face of lies, his speech that cut through all pretense, his tender engagement with those who hurt. And now "the Man" stands at the Father's right hand interceding for us,[24] for he knows our need for wisdom first-hand. The Father delights to send the wisdom from on high that has wondrously been "domesticated" (for lack of humanly accessible language) in the incarnate life of his Son. A human mind once carried unhindered wisdom from above. Now the Holy Spirit can fill simple souls who are hungry for such wisdom with the mind that is, indeed, ours in Christ

Jesus. What a dance of initiative and response, giving and receiving and giving again!

Who would not be eager to receive such a gift? Yet the tragedy I see is that godly wisdom is so often lacking in Christian contexts. We often seem to suffer from a split between spiritual life and practical planning. Do we fear that if we ask God for specific wisdom it will impede the progress of our good strategic planning models? I suspect that wisdom is often perceived as an inconvenient and impractical distraction, guaranteed to insert a stick in the wheel of a fast moving vehicle. Whatever we do, we don't want to stop. So we keep moving, but our progress often looks more like a wave of the sea, driven and tossed by the wind,[25] than an intentional trip to be discerned step by step.

Wisdom does not impede the movement of the vehicle. Instead, she whispers. She says, "If any of you lacks wisdom, let him ask God, who gives generously to all without reproach, and it will be given him."[26] Asking in faith for godly wisdom in concrete contexts changes the trajectory of our reliance. Rather than looking down into our circumstances for our answers, we move forward with our heads up and our ears tuned to hear a voice that is rarely raised. Ironically, only God-given wisdom prevents our wheels from spinning, makes clear the path before us, and grants us thoughtful creativity and humble joy along the way. Is not "establish the work of our hands for us"[27] a prayer that the wisdom from above be effectively and beautifully delivered into the real contexts of our lives?

The Crown Jewel

I tasted wisdom's practical beauty in the early stages of writing this book. Within a two-week period several emails appeared in my inbox from women who had taken my *Women in the Kingdom* course when it was first offered at Wheaton in the mid-nineties. Now, ten years later, these women, in one way or another, approached me with a similar request. "Carla, I'm in a completely different place in my life than I was when I took your course at Wheaton. I really need wisdom. Would you consider re-connecting with me?" And, I—delighted to find these thirty-something women hungering for nourishing conversation—joyfully placed my heart, my home, and a blog site at their service for a season.

I learned much from these women who, a decade since I had first met them, were found in such diverse worlds as legal offices, inner city ministries, modeling agencies, accounting firms, hospitals, theater productions, marriage and motherhood. We gathered once a month to talk about life, study the Scriptures together, and pray for each other. I watched humility and meekness form as these younger sisters of mine shared their struggles and asked searching questions. I watched them grow in sincerity and in the ability to consider perspectives they had not yet entertained as they sought to walk their diverse paths in godly ways. Wisdom was being formed among us, and she was lovely, indeed.

I have come to understand wisdom as the crown jewel of these songs of assent. We are not specifically instructed to pray for simplicity, although it is the exquisitely freeing fruit of a heart that is enabled to say, "you choose for me—I trust you." And receptivity is the foundational motion of the redeemed soul as our gate is opened to receive the good seed of all God's manifold graces. In the chapters to come, we will see confidence and buoyancy as two specific in-graced responses to the soul's "yes" to God that are, in their own ways, an extension of wisdom's lovely fruit.

But wisdom holds a unique place among our in-graced responses to God's love. To open the gate of one's soul to "the wisdom from above" is to receive a gift that bears a specific name, and a very particular signature. Wisdom, and all the good fruit that proceeds from her, may well be considered the crown jewel of all that is feminine. For wisdom is sought, received, held and extended by the same name. She is both grace from above and response to that grace. We are diligently to seek her and are promised that, in so doing, we will gain great reward,[28] including peace with God, self and others,[29] insight into life, and even the Lord's favor.[30] He who is the great initiator of favor toward dependent creatures continues to bless them as they turn their faces up toward his own.

No wonder wisdom is marked by characteristics like purity, peace, and gentleness; reasonableness, mercy, impartiality and sincerity. Her presence produces so many good fruits in the lives of others that James celebrates her as the benefactress of a "harvest of righteousness."[31] Wisdom is God's grace springing up very close to the ground.

Deception from Below

Yet, even as we bask in the beauty of godly wisdom received from above, we dare not ignore wisdom's inherent challenge. For, while all true wisdom is received, not all that is received is wise. Having considered the creativity and beauty of godly wisdom, we also need to think well about wisdom's toxic imitation.

One evening our small women's fellowship was engaged in a Bible Study when two new women appeared at my door well over an hour after the meeting had begun. They were acquaintances of one of the group's members and I welcomed them in, attempting to help them acclimate to the gentle, transparent tone that graced our time together that evening.

But our visitors had another agenda. One of them informed us that "the Lord had told her" to tell her story that night. She proceeded to take over the group with a rather voyeuristic testimony. Then her friend chimed in with a set of equally inappropriate comments that overtly attacked these women that she had never met.

I found myself speechless. I would like to believe I would handle the situation very differently now, but at the time I didn't know what to do, and, as I admitted to my friends later on, when I don't know what to do, I tend to withdraw from potential conflict. The best I could do at the moment was quickly to bring the meeting to a close. The visitors, along with their shocked and mortified friend from our group, left soon afterwards.

In the days to come I began to realize how deeply wounding the intrusion had been to the women in attendance that night.

The group's collective gate had been flung wide open—they had been sharing honestly with each other as they were drinking deeply from the Scriptures. The interruption was experienced as a violation of something vital and holy, as was made abundantly clear by the ensuing emails and phone calls from several members of the group.

Soon after this poisonous episode I met with the group member who had invited these women. Her "friends" had indicated an interest in women's ministry, and she thought this group would bless them. She was as appalled as the rest of us at what had actually occurred.

What had happened here? Two women walked into my home with their own, self-absorbed agenda, broke all the socially appropriate rules of being a good guest, and forced their will on the rest of the group. This would not be the kind of "spirit" desirable in any context. But because this was a moment when the group's collective gate was wide open to the Lord and to each other, it was experienced as far more extreme than mere rudeness. The "fruit" of their visit was confusion, fear, anger and a strong temptation to withdraw from the group as a whole on the part of some of its most sensitive members.

In Folly's Room

We were visited by Dame Folly that evening. She injected the room with poison.

> The woman Folly is loud;
>
> she is seductive and knows nothing.
>
> She sits at the door of her house;

she takes a seat on the highest places of the town,

calling to those who pass by,

who are going straight on their way,

"Whoever is simple, let him turn in here!"

And to him who lacks sense she says,

"Stolen water is sweet,

and bread eaten in secret is pleasant."

But he does not know that the dead are there,

that her guests are in the depths of Sheol.[32]

While Lady Wisdom is carefully laying the foundation for a nourishing meal, Dame Folly does nothing but sit and shout. She knows nothing about the responsive creativity of wisdom. If my unknown guests had come into my home, sat quietly for a time and listened to the conversation already underway, discerned the tone of the meeting, and monitored their own internal thoughts as to what would be helpful and loving to share in that context, they might have offered a wise insight or two. But no creativity is required for those who move from place to place in a manner that distracts people from the real thing going on quietly in their midst. Words come prepackaged. Actions are rehearsed in advance.

This is Dame Folly, who simultaneously sits at the door of her house and does nothing, and also takes a seat in the highest places of the town where she can attract attention to herself with her loud invitation for others to join her. In the case of our women's group, the contrast between wisdom and folly was quite evident.

But often the contrast is less obvious—at least on the surface. In Proverbs 9, Lady Wisdom and Dame Folly issue precisely the same invitation. The *voice* is different, but the *words* are exactly the same. "Whoever is simple, let him turn in here!"[33]

I am reminded of Frodo Baggins, the brave little hobbit in the *Lord of Rings*, who, together with his companions, must discern if a certain "ranger" offering himself as a guide to the company is good or evil. Having just recently stepped onto the road to wisdom himself, Frodo hesitantly observed,

> You have frightened me several times tonight, but never in the way that servants of the Enemy would, or so I imagine. I think one of his spies would—well, seem fairer and feel fouler, if you understand.[34]

How much we, with Tolkien's little hobbit, need to understand the difference in that which "seems fair but feels fouler." As the prophecy that surrounded Frodo's good, but rugged, ranger proclaimed, "All that is gold does not glitter."[35] Dame Folly glitters. She seems fair. But she is foul; no golden strand is ever found within her.

One of the characteristics of that which seems fair but feels foul is the unwillingness to be patient enough to prepare a meal worthy of open invitation. Folly is lazy. She does not even draw her own water. She just steals that which belongs to someone else. And folly is deceptive. She prefers private liaisons where her bread can be eaten in secret. No intentional purpose. No discerning community.

No concern for anyone but herself. Only death reigns in her house. For her to invite others to join her at her place is like handing them a letter filled with the anthrax virus. They will die. But she does not care. Her signature is self-absorption masked in the manipulation of others to achieve her own purposes.

Deception's Disease

If these characteristics of spiritual deception were confined to "Dame Folly" in the book of Proverbs we could move quickly away from her door. But she is all too heartbreakingly present in our day. For while some things feel as foul as they are, there is a much more seductive form of folly. Here deception begins by embracing something that initially looks quite attractive. The descent into folly is a progressive disease. None of us are fully in touch with the desires of our hearts—and none of us are endowed with natural spiritual immunities against such deception. The Lord is far more interested in cultivating our dependence on him than in sparing us the struggle. "Lord, have mercy" is intended to emanate upward from within our souls with great regularity.

To be in touch with the good human desires of one's own heart is a lovely gift. Our human desires propel us forward in many ways that are essential to life. Because we are creatures who desire, we learn, we grow, we taste, we touch, we long to know and be known by others…we live.

But when the desires of our hearts are mistaken for the voice of God, we find ourselves inching down a path of counterfeit wisdom. Job has a very apt description of this potential confusion. During his final appeal before God, throughout which Job continues to defend his innocence in the midst of calamity, he utters these words: "if my step has turned aside from the way and my heart has gone after my eyes..."[36] I would suggest that it is perfectly possible for our hearts to go after our eyes and to mistake what we then see through our clouded vision as wisdom from God.

These spiritual cataracts, like their physical counterparts, are formed over time and slowly obstruct the passage of light. The spiritual strain often begins with a mental activity that seems innocuous enough at first. It's just an escapist fantasy. Perhaps I like to imagine a future in which I am successful and well known. Perhaps I prefer to imagine a place where no demands are placed upon me or ultimate comfort is immediately within reach. Or, perhaps I escape into an imaginary relationship where I am admired and adored—by a fictitious someone who never argues with me, always finds me interesting and does precisely whatever I ask of him. This latter fantasy may or may not be spun around a real person, but the relationship I spin in my mind has no bearing on reality. And it can swiftly become an affair of the heart. Such a fantasy is dangerous to my soul because it renders me increasingly incapable of living inside real relationship in my rather unremarkable everyday life.

Of course, flights of imagination are not always debilitating. This past January I spent three glorious hours on the Atlantic coast on a cloudless, eighty-degree Wednesday at low-tide. I saw only three people on the beach during those three hours (my admittedly selfish idea of paradise). I spent the time picking up shells that actually required me to select a color palate to guide my selections because there were so many different varieties for the choosing. Now, months later, I still go back to God's gracious gift of a Wednesday afternoon at the beach, and the memory continues to renew me.

But an escapist fantasy, whether of imaginary power, place, or lover, will not renew my soul. Rather, such a fantasy slowly strangles the life out of my daily existence like a cataract blocking light. The poisonous effect of an escapist fantasy is greed and lust, increasing my desire to want what is not there for the taking. Furthermore, such a fantasy is stamped with two essential fingerprints: I am always the person at the center of an escapist fantasy and I become increasingly discontent with my real life the longer I live in my imaginary world.

There is a dangerous compulsivity to these hidden fantasies that entrap us the longer we live in them. Our increasing inability to turn from these thoughts is the mark of the enemy's foothold in our hearts. For when we nurse these fantasies we willingly, albeit naïvely, open the door and lay out the welcome mat for a more direct enemy invasion.

The Lord will not enter in here. He passes through real doors, not illusory ones. He will beckon us to come and join him out where the air is clean and the light is bright. But escapist fantasies must be killed by suffocation. We have to abandon them and let them die for lack of air. If they are not too deeply rooted we may be able to walk away from them on our own. But the insidious dynamic of such fantasies is that they thrive in darkness. If they have become deeply rooted in our souls, we may well need to expose them to the light in the presence of a mature Christian sister or brother in order to come free.

I have been walking alongside a friend who is struggling to suffocate the escapist fantasy of living in an imaginary relationship with a real man to whom she had begun to give her heart. Living in a challenging marriage, this imaginary relationship had become far more attractive to her than her real, painful life. When she first shared this development in her thinking with me she had no idea of the trap in which she was caught. She did know that she was confused and lacked the wisdom to know how to walk in her real life. Thankfully, we had established a relationship based on a desire for discerning God's wisdom, and she was humble enough to hear my concerns and grateful to be returned to reality. She is back in a place where she can walk the hard road she is on with the Lord shedding his light on her next step. Sadly, I know other Christian women who have lived in such escapist fantasies so long and so deeply that they will not relinquish their hidden affair. There is absolutely no room for true wisdom to be established in the midst of this kind of self-absorption.

The Cure of Clarity

St. Bernard of Clairveaux once made the observation that "a wise man is one who savors all things as they really are."[37] As our eyes are made clear by God's sustaining grace, we are given the increased capacity to perceive simple truth, beauty and goodness. With sparkling vision we can go for a simple walk and rejoice in creation's praise. We can watch young children at play and love their spontaneous laughter. And, most important of all, we begin increasingly to discern real wisdom from her counterfeit because we are honestly facing our own hearts. We grow increasingly aware of our vulnerabilities. We are, then, enabled to come to our Lord as creatures dependent on him for the clarity of our spiritual sight and are thus increasingly able to perceive the difference between truth and illusion.

The spiritual discipline of facing where our thoughts go when left to themselves and turning away from them simultaneously sets our feet in the way of wisdom. Without any striving, our lives then begin to take on the characteristics of Lady Wisdom. The qualities of the humble, transparent life that she offers enable us to go quietly about our real lives, graciously opening our heart's gate to others who want to taste the goodness on which we feast. We pass wisdom on, investing in our neighbor while walking whatever path lies open before us to do so. And, to the extent that we are the vessels of Lady Wisdom, she is able to serve a nourishing banquet so that those who come and eat can "leave their simple ways and live" and, together with us, "walk in the way of insight."

Super-Spiritual Blindness

Just as physical cataracts proceed down a slow path to blindness, our spiritual cataracts can take a similar turn. If our unruly hearts are permitted to go after our eyes, the disease cannot only manifest itself as an unfruitful escape from our everyday lives, but as a gradual entrée into spiritual unreality as well. And while super-spirituality may seem relatively innocuous, it is actually quite insidious. The damage that can be done to our souls and our communities has the potential to be unspeakably destructive. Without the input of other Christians who can help us discern the difference between God's voice and the voice of our own hearts, we can easily find ourselves stumbling in the darkness.

Consider, again, the characteristics of Dame Folly. She is passive and frenetic at the same time. She cleverly avoids the daily activities of life by appearing to be busy with more "spiritual" ones. When she's not sitting at the door of her own house she is making loud, distracting claims of "wisdom" to those who pass by. Real Christian wisdom will make us more human and more able to enter into the normal activities of life. It will never disconnect us from those activities. Ironically, in the midst of her swing between passivity and activism, Dame Folly's goal is not really about the activities themselves. Rather, her intent is to draw attention to herself. She is so completely self-absorbed that she will go to any means necessary to be seen.

This desperate need to be noticed is the unseen dynamic under so much of the counterfeit wisdom manifesting itself in our day. And while I have not explored this dangerous dynamic in depth with my brothers in Christ, I have spent a great deal of time with Christian women who have been entrapped in counterfeit wisdom in former seasons of life. This is what I hear: "I was the special, cute, adored daughter. As I grew up, I expected that God would adore me, too. I needed to be 'special' to him. I had no place to put the possibility that I was actually pretty normal, but that God dearly loved me anyway. So I sought for ways to continue to be special to God."

Or, from the opposite extreme, "I always felt invisible. I wanted to be noticed so badly. And so, rather than living in the kind of real relationship to Jesus that is grounded in everyday life and lived with others in Christian community, I developed a kind of spiritual affair…just my god and me. I wouldn't describe it as 'personal,' it was, rather, a private and secret relationship. Only a few other 'initiated' people could understand what I was really experiencing."

In neither case did these women understand the nature of God's unmerited favor and unyielding love. Instead, out of their confusion, need and sin, they began to mirror Dame Folly's insistence that "bread eaten in secret is pleasant."[38]

One of the major dynamics of counterfeit wisdom in our day is the claim to a specialized knowledge for which only a few have "the gift."[39] Over the years I have learned to close my internal gate quickly when a person with whom I have no sustained relationship says to me, "I have a word from the Lord for you." It is generally far more about the need of the messenger than the recipient. As a fellow Christian once told a former "messenger" as she related a "word" she been given for someone else, "That has about as much power as a stick of gum." This is often the best that can be said about such words. But the power of these words to confuse and to harm is much more serious.

Tragically, one of the signatures of Dame Folly's descendents is an unwillingness to have these words tested in community. If you are drinking "stolen water," you really don't want it traced to its source. While real wisdom is humble and "open to reason,"[40] counterfeit wisdom is neither humble nor reasonable. It prefers a pedestal—an exalted place from which it can deliver its messages without taking responsibility for the bitter fruit it produces.

Because the seeds of counterfeit wisdom spring out of the prideful need to be "special," weeds of confusion, fear, envy and slander quickly overtake communities that fail to perceive the destructive element here. A counterfeit "word from the lord" with its source in selfish ambition is indeed, as James observes, "demonic,"[41] and will make the people of God ill. Some will run after this counterfeit wisdom themselves, infected by the desire to be "special" as well, grasping for what is not theirs to take, while others will be paralyzed by confusion or fear, trying to discern what really is true. Sadly, the people are not protected when leaders cannot recognize or confront the difference between the wisdom that enables us to "walk in the way of insight" and its counterfeit that, in the end, produces nothing but death.

And while the community suffers greatly, in the end, those caught in the self-deception of counterfeit wisdom are in the most serious danger. For a private affair with a god of our own making whose name happens to be Jesus is the worst form of an escapist fantasy. It is not real relationship with the true God.

As we will see in the next chapter, the Lord loves us with a love that is personal, but not private. In the Gospels Jesus regularly engages women in significant conversations and then points them outward into grounded, everyday life.[42] He sends the woman at the well back to her community and he tells a repentant prostitute to go in peace and sin no more. Likewise, he will not let Mary Magdalene cling to him after his resurrection, but sends her back to the brothers with a real message from their Lord, a word that does not draw attention to her in any way. All of these women know that they are known and loved by Jesus, yet the knowing and loving consistently produces solid good for the sake of others. Nothing the counterfeit produces is remotely comparable.

If counterfeit wisdom is the path our hearts are permitted to tread, we can develop serious spiritual cataracts. Our internal vision will become cloudy and, if our hearts are allowed to persist in this way, our eyes, the body's lamp, will grow increasingly full of darkness.[43]

Among the people of God, no one is in more potential danger of succumbing to Dame Folly's seductions than those who desire deeply to have a "relationship" with God and are spiritually sensitive (or even just has an active imagination), but have no wise, outside voices to help them discern the difference between the needs of their own hearts and the voice of the Lord. There are those in the church who truly desire to love Jesus (or perhaps more truthfully, to know themselves loved by him), yet are literally losing their minds because those around them are unable to distinguish between true and counterfeit wisdom.

As I write I have before me the faces of three precious women who have gone down this dreadful path. One was rescued just on this side of completely losing her sanity, and one is walking the long path back from a mental breakdown. It has taken years for these two friends to have their soul's scaffolding rebuilt in such a way that they can entrust themselves to true communion with the living God. I find it instructive that both of them are now marked by a foundational awareness of their complete dependence on God to discern between reality and illusion. Tragically, the third precious one is, as I write, totally unable to perceive reality. She is entirely encased in her super-spiritualized self-absorption. Perceiving herself to be a woman of great spiritual wisdom, and surrounded by a small circle who confirm her in this deception, she does not realize that those closest to her do not receive life, but rather have life drained from them. She has become a terrifying specter of Dame Folly.

And while I speak with particular passion to my sisters in Christ, my brothers are not immune. Their particular fingerprint more often emerges as a compulsive desire for power than a craving need for intimacy. I still teach in a world where pastors can be put on pedestals, and I tell my men that the worst path they could go down is actually to believe what their admirers tell them about themselves. Self-admiration is just another name for self-absorption, and super-spirituality is not the exclusive domain of women. Dame Folly has no problem appearing in masculine guise. His name is Lucifer.

The Cure of Godly Fear

But God is so gracious, and ever sends wisdom's quiet chorale to sing to the confused hearts of his people. The words are ancient: "the fear of the Lord is the beginning of wisdom."[44] There are two kinds of fear—both of which have their place along the path of wisdom. The first is to desire wisdom so that we will avoid trouble. Many of the actual proverbs have this kind of tone. For example, "The prudent man sees danger and hides himself, but the simple go on and suffer for it."[45] Such a proverb draws a clear distinction between the actions of the wise and the foolish, between the outcomes of life and death.

The second kind of fear is the desire to do nothing that will displease the one we are made to please. This latter "fear of the Lord" will sustain us when our "wounded surgeon plies the steel"[46] and cuts deeply in order to remove even the slightest spiritual cataract. The temptation to get off the operating table may be strong. But if we seek wisdom "like silver and search for it as for hidden treasures,"[47] then we will not shrink from the Great Physician's knife. Learning obedience from what we suffer has been tried and not found wanting.

In Christian Community's House

Because true wisdom is such a glorious gift from God, we ought not be surprised at the destructive power of its counterfeit. But we are not to be paralyzed by such a reality—only humbled. One dimension of the "fear of the Lord" that is the beginning of wisdom is recognizing our very real capacity to self-deceive. Coming to understand one's own soul in this manner is the first step along the path of true wisdom. I wonder if this acknowledgement of the possibility of self-deception is one of the reasons James introduces wisdom as "meek."[48] One of my favorite definitions of meekness is allowing others to say about you what you privately would acknowledge to be true before the face of God. This willingness to be examined, to live and act in the light of Christian community, is fundamental if we are truly to carry wisdom from above.

One of my students recently related to me a rich example of godly wisdom emerging from Christian community. She had been through a painful divorce involving business entanglements that, after several years, were not yet fully resolved. And she had recently become engaged. After the couple had set a wedding date a friend of hers gently suggested that the timing of the wedding might be too soon. My student was initially very angry, but didn't completely dismiss the conversation. And then her pastor lovingly likened her life to the liturgical year. Her life had metaphorically passed through Advent, Christmas, Epiphany and Lent, but, as a result of the pain of her divorce, she had been stuck in Good Friday for a very long time. She had not yet experienced Easter, nor the long summer of "common time." Perhaps the couple would be wise to wait a season before remarrying. After some weeks of struggle, she and her fiancé came to peace with their community's loving recommendation. She freely admitted that, even in waiting, she would still have to face the effects of her former marriage. And I said, "Yes, but you will have the blessing of your community behind you. That is an incomparable strength."

My friend is learning the grace of godly, practical wisdom formed in community. For nothing is so humbling as yielding to the wisdom of our community of faith when our heart is saying something else. And yet I have no doubt that she and her fiancé will experience the blessing of the real peace and clarity that can only be established in God's people as we walk in humility before God and with each other. Neither do I doubt that she will grow in the wisdom that will increase her own godly perceptiveness for the future good of others. The mutuality of receiving and extending God-given wisdom is one of Christ's fingerprints in vital Christian community.

As the decisions in need of godly wisdom impact the lives of more people, so does the need for a multiplicity of godly counselors. Spiritual discernment is not to be limited to visible and vocal leaders alone. In reality, because of all the complicated factors that bombard leaders, they may be the least able to receive wisdom directly from above at any given moment. But if they are wise, they will be grateful for godly counsel, for "a word fitly spoken is like apples of gold in a setting of silver."[49]

Discernment is the responsibility of the whole community, but especially of those whose lives increasingly yield the treasure of the wisdom from above. It ought not be surprising that such lives will be marked the priorities that Jesus carried—love for neighbor, forgiveness of enemies, gratitude for all simple gifts, thankfulness for being caught up in Jesus' access to the Father.

They will be increasingly shaped by our Lord's inwardly digested humility, mercy and care for the poor. One can be "elder" in Christ's church without necessarily being publicly identified as one. Blessed, indeed, is the church that has a few godly elders— perhaps especially when they are not standing up front.

The Great Reversal Revisited

In G.K. Chesterton's masterpiece, *St. Francis of Assisi*, he describes the spiritual giftedness of St. Francis as that of a juggler who perceived the world aright because he chose to engage it while standing on his spiritual head. Sometimes one sees more clearly from that angle. To hold fast to the position that any wisdom worth having is not simply the natural result of age, experience or giftedness, but real content that descends from the Father by the virtue of his Son through the grace-filled ministry of the Holy Spirit has something of the same flavor. Mary's *Magnificat* anticipated this scrambled up perspective where those who believe they are wise are brought low, and those who know their "humble estate" are raised up.

The treasure of such wisdom is always held in a chest of humility. To begin by knowing that one does not know, to digest and quietly offer what one comes to know, to walk close enough to the ground to know what is worth knowing, and to test and share that knowing with others—how could one part Lady Wisdom from handmaiden humility? Perhaps T.S. Eliot said it best,

> The only wisdom we can hope to acquire
>
> Is the wisdom of humility: humility is endless.[50]

Confidence

And when the time came for their purification according to the Law of Moses, they brought him up to Jerusalem to present him to the Lord (as it is written in the Law of the Lord, "Every male who first opens the womb shall be called holy to the Lord") and to offer a sacrifice according to what is said in the Law of the Lord, "a pair of turtledoves, or two young pigeons." Now there was a man in Jerusalem, whose name was Simeon, and this man was righteous and devout, waiting for the consolation of Israel, and the Holy Spirit was upon him. And it had been revealed to him by the Holy Spirit that he would not see death before he had seen the Lord's Christ. And he came in the Spirit into the temple, and when the parents brought in the child Jesus, to do for him according to the custom of the Law, he took him up in his arms and blessed God and said, "Lord, now you are letting your servant depart in peace, according to your word; for my eyes have seen your salvation that you have prepared in the presence of all peoples, a light for revelation to the Gentiles, and for glory to your people Israel." And his father and his mother marveled at what was said about him. And Simeon blessed them and said to Mary his mother, "Behold, this child is appointed for the fall and rising of many in Israel, and for a sign that is opposed (and a sword will pierce through your own soul also), so that thoughts from many hearts may be revealed." (Luke 2: 22-35)

"A Sword Will Pierce Your Soul"

For an old man waiting for the consolation of Israel, his words to Mary were anything but comforting. Propelled by the Holy Spirit into the temple on this particular day, Simeon had honed right in on this small, poor family. Catching Jesus up in his arms, Simeon blessed God and spoke of the destiny of the child while Mary and Joseph marveled at the old man's powerful pronouncement. But then, after blessing the parents, Simeon looked right at Mary and, mid-sentence, declared, "a sword will pierce your own soul also."[1]

I wonder if Mary experienced these words more as a confirmation than a prophecy. Her faithful Joseph stood beside her on that day of purification, yet there had been an earlier day when he had not understood and in the midst of making plans to divorce her she had spoken no words to defend herself.[2] We do not know how her village reacted to her pregnancy, but we do know that she hastened to see Elizabeth and didn't come home in a hurry.[3] By the time Simeon spoke she was existentially living her "humble estate," having just given birth to Jesus in surroundings that were certainly not what she would have desired for this child. And only a short time later, she would flee to Egypt with Joseph and Jesus—isolated refugees leaving the carnage of dead children in their wake.[4] Her heart must already have begun to sting.

But there is a second way in which Mary would experience that sword dangling in front of her heart. This time it was wielded not by her circumstances, but by this very son. Jesus was the fulfillment of the prophet Isaiah's word, "He made my mouth like a sharp sword..."[5] This sword pressed close when Mary, finding Jesus in the temple, said to him, "Your father and I have been searching for you in great distress," and Jesus' response to her was, "Did you not know I must be in my Father's house?"[6] Mary treasured up all these things in her heart and a merciful veil comes down over the life of this family. For the next eighteen years we are told only that Jesus "increased in wisdom and in stature and in favor with God and man."[7]

During those hidden years Mary must also have increased in wisdom as she came to know the heart of the Father as it was manifest in her son. His increased self-understanding must surely have translated into even more spiritual treasure for her own heart to ponder. She would have need of such confidence in the face of her own lonely journey. Years later, when Jesus returned to his native Nazareth to preach, her neighbors welcomed him home by attempting to throw him off a cliff.[8] His life was imperiled long before he was impaled on the cross, and the sword prophesied for his mother probed her heart long before it pierced her through.

Her son would soon be telling his disciples that they needed to take up their cross and follow him,[9] but Mary's own unique expression of discipleship had already been established—she was not to run away from the sword that loomed right in front of her eyes. Mary did not waver. She remained present to him, even when her mind did not understand. "The mother's vision is unequal to that of her son, but her heart, like chosen ground, is deep enough to sustain the highest tree."[10]

The Father had fortified Mary in each new "Amen" of her receptive heart. And under the cross we catch a final glimpse of a heart that had lived "let it be to me" for a very long time. When released at the foot of her son's cross into the home of another,[11] she bore without flinching the final thrust that parted her flesh from his. That sword pierced tissue soft yet strong—for by this time Mary's heart had been tempered by a quiet confidence that can only be forged in fire.

Do You See This Woman?

Sinners

If I shut my eyes, I can still remember the morning after. My son was an "all-boy" two-year-old, and, escaping my grasp, had run out into a dark shopping center parking lot the night before. I was angry, I was tired, and I experienced a moment of utter terror for my child. So I took him home and spanked him—with a wooden spoon. And in the morning, as I was dressing him, I found the spoon marks my anger had left behind.

I was devastated. Years earlier I had worked with teenage mothers and had, more than once, faced issues of child abuse. But in this particular moment I was confronted with the reality that I was completely capable of the same behavior. I felt naked and deeply ashamed. I wanted to hide from everyone—my husband, my son, my baby sitter and my God. And I could hide from none of them. But God, in his mercy, gave me the grace to come to him in my private agony.

As I confessed my sin, a passage from Isaiah 61 came slowly rising from the depths of my soul:

> I will greatly rejoice in the Lord;
>
> My soul shall exult in my God,
>
> For he has clothed me with the garments of salvation;
>
> He has covered me with the robe of righteousness.[12]

And in that moment the truth went *in*. I saw my Lord, with the shadow of the cross and empty tomb behind him, wrapping his own robe around my nakedness and raising me up. He took my hand and led me to the throne of his Father and said, "Father, do you see this woman? She belongs to you." In that moment I was released from my paralyzing guilt and shame and tasted what it meant to be covered by a righteousness that was not of my own making. "For our sake God made him to be sin who knew no sin, so that in him we might become the righteousness of God."[13] My head had known what it meant to be granted access to the Father through a righteousness not my own. Now my heart began to wear that reality.

But the lesson continued. Not long after this transforming experience I found myself in a setting where I had been designated the court jester. In the mocking that ensued I found myself assigned a ragged costume that did not fit me. During several long months of being derided as a fool, I needed to know the Lord's protection of me, for I had no way to protect myself. My very tangible ride up an elevator became holy ground. As the elevator rose through the floors, I would, with the eyes of my heart, see the Lord placing his robe of protection on me as though I was being lifted up into it. I would step onto my floor in the knowledge that his robe completely covered me. During those fiery months, I learned just how safe I was within his covering. The mocking could wound, but it could not destroy me as long as I remained hidden in him.

One more hard lesson sealed this radical truth of being clothed in a righteousness not my own. This time, I was neither naked nor wearing a ragged costume forced on me by others. I was, instead, clad in spiritual sackcloth. After all kinds of turmoil, I had stepped out of a community that I dearly loved. I was hurting and so were they. But, in some respects, I was wiser now.

I knew as I was leaving that I would not walk the long road before me with anything approaching perfection. I was no longer under any illusions that I had any righteousness of my own to contribute to the situation. And as I pondered what it meant to be clothed in Christ during this season, I came to understand myself to be held close and safe and, at the same time, to live in a garment as billowy and expansive as a large tent. I did not have to fear movement within it. I could rest in the Lord's righteousness and walk my all-too-human road. He had me covered—my job was to walk with my head lifted up to receive light for the step right in front of me.

Another Sinner

One of my sisters in the communion of saints would surely be smiling if she were standing over my shoulder reading this story. She, too, was a sinful, rejected, hurting woman. In her desperation she crashed a dinner party given by a Pharisee named Simon.[14] As a prostitute, she would not have been in the habit of entering into respectable homes. But she knew that Jesus was inside. He had just proclaimed that he was a friend of sinners, and she believed him. He had already cleansed the body of an unclean leper and healed the soul as well as the body of a paralytic man. He'd called a tax collector to follow him. Perhaps, she thought, he would even love women like her. Starved for such love, she broke all the rules and entered the room.

We don't know if this woman had ever encountered Jesus first-hand before this moment. I am inclined to think not. I think she walked into that room and was utterly undone by the love that radiated from Jesus as his grace-filled face of welcome turned her direction. She had never encountered a man who so freely welcomed a compromised woman, for Jesus' initial response neither shunned nor objectified her. She went to stand behind him as he was reclining at the table, and his response to her completely deflected the inhospitable reactions in the rest of the room.

Whatever her prior contact with Jesus, she didn't come prepared for what actually happened. Her ointment would have been part of the tools of her trade, but what woman plans to weep hard enough to wash someone's feet with her tears? It was all so spontaneous. As her tears were dropping on his feet the only towel at her disposal was her hair. So, while voluntarily letting down her hair in public was a complete breach of rabbinic propriety (where the loosing of hair was a way of disgracing a suspected adulteress),[15] her spontaneous act now served a very practical purpose. Due to Simon's ambivalence toward Jesus, the most elemental form of hospitality had been overlooked. Jesus' feet had not been washed. But this oversight was soon remedied. My sister's tears washed away the dirt. Her hair finished wiping his feet clean. By this time she was kneeling on the floor, kissing and anointing Jesus' feet as she conveyed her gratitude in response to his overwhelming love.

In the midst of the appalled silence that ensued around the table, I can imagine Jesus quietly reaching behind him and gently laying his hand on her head, enabling her to soak in acceptance born of being fully known and completely loved, as well as that yet unnamed something else that was his forgiveness of her sins.

By the time Jesus actually opened his mouth, all the dramatic action on her part had already occurred. Only then did Jesus ask Simon the question that cut through the pretense in the room and schooled the Pharisees in their own tradition. God never despises a broken and contrite heart.[16]

Jesus asked Simon, "Do you see this woman?" And as the incarnate "God of seeing"[17] turned and looked into her eyes, he pronounced his blessing upon all her actions toward him. Then he spoke the word that, even unspoken, had been washing over her in waves of joy from the moment she walked into the room: "your sins are forgiven." Finally, in the midst of the muttered incredulity behind him at the table, Jesus spoke the benediction that opened her life to a freedom she had never known. "Your faith has saved you; go in peace."[18]

The robe Jesus placed on me was woven from his righteousness. My first-century sister was wrapped in Jesus' peace. Yet, before either of us could wear such beautiful clothing, internal surgery had to be performed. We had first to encounter our Lord as healer. This unnamed woman knelt before our incarnate Christ; my heart opened to receive the ministry of his Holy Spirit. Our sins were forgiven, our wounds were cleansed, and our fears were lifted. For neither Jesus in his earthly ministry nor the Holy Spirit sent forth in his name will have anything to do with merely covering up nakedness, ill-fitting costumes or sackcloth. If we would be made a new creation, our debilitating brokenness and sin must first be lifted off of us by Christ's healing power. For when we are covered by Jesus' righteousness or wrapped in his peace, we are meant to live in a spacious place of freedom where we learn to walk, run and occasionally even soar as we gratefully wear beautiful garments that are not of our own making.

Living within Jesus' robe of righteousness has become a very tangible gift to my internal sight. For me, this robe is made out of the lightest fabric possible, yet is as strong as steel. Tolkien's "mithral coat" that clad Frodo in *Lord of the Rings* has certainly influenced me here: "the silver corslet shimmered before his eyes like the light upon a rippling sea…the sound of the shaken rings were like the tinkle of rain in a pool."[19] The robe I see is pure white on the outside and blood red on the inside. It has a long train and a cross at its back. The hood of the robe protects my mind, while the beautiful, strong material is crossed in a double-layer over my heart, gathered at each shoulder. It is, quite honestly, most unusual for me to "see" such a thing in such vivid detail. But I know beyond any doubt that the only way to live in such a way that I am receptive to God and responsive to him in this world is to allow my heart to be wrapped in the protection of Jesus. And so I wear his robe confidently, knowing that I do not, nor ever shall, wear a righteousness of my own, but that as long as I remain in Christ I am protected and have no need to fear.

If we would be made whole, our hearts need something we can see to enter into realities that would otherwise elude us.[20] The angel approached Mary with a word picture—"the power of the Most High will overshadow you." Simeon affirmed reality for Mary by painting her another picture—"a sword will pierce your soul." And, following a similar pattern, the Spirit came to me with the picture my own heart needed—"he has covered me with a robe of righteousness."

But our hearts need stories as well as pictures. Jesus' interactions with broken human beings are not only true in that they actually happened, but true in their power to reveal Jesus as the "Christ, the Son of the living God." To believe and be given life in his name[21] is as present a reality now as it was to those women and men healed in the Gospels with whom we are invited to identify so deeply that they might as well come home with us for dinner.

Jesus' arm is mighty enough to touch a woman kneeling on the floor next to him while extending that same hand to a hurting soul two millennia later. In some lives, both then and now, grateful confidence in Jesus' love, healing and protection is poured into us in a single epiphany.

Friends

But in other lives such confidence in God unfolds over a longer period. The Gospels record one such story as it is related in three separate vignettes. It is the tale of two sisters—Martha and Mary. Luke introduces us to these sisters of Lazarus at the end of chapter 10 in his Gospel, and then their stories are picked up again in chapters 11 and 12 of the Gospel of John. The sustained interaction of each sister with Jesus enables us to glimpse his creative work in each one and to dwell upon the different expressions of confidence in their Lord that were born from these life-changing encounters. Perhaps we will find that, just as Jesus met these first century friends, by His Spirit, he will also delight to meet us.

Martha

We are often so closely bound by our need to control others that we don't see what we are doing. We set up all our loved ones on a chessboard and move them around like pieces that need to progress in a certain way according to what we think is best for them. But Jesus doesn't play chess very well. He keeps messing up the board. Whether it is what he says or when he arrives, he moves according to a logic beyond any attempt at human control.

To my mind Martha[22] is the feminine counterpart to Peter. She didn't leap out of boats to be the first one on shore, but she shared his gift of eager impulsiveness. Her particular strategy was to lay first claim to Bethany's hospitality rights for Jesus.

In their first encounter, Martha's hospitable head was no doubt filled with plans for getting her home spotless and a fabulous meal prepared—only the best for Jesus. But when Mary failed to cooperate with Martha's carefully designed program, Marth'a restless heart shot out from behind her carefully crafted details. And when she protested her sister's lack of cooperation, Jesus caught her boomerang and tossed it right back at her.

But Martha trusted Jesus. And when Lazarus died and Jesus finally showed up outside the village, Martha went out to meet him there, this time full of the intense pain at her brother's death and her Lord's apparent callousness.[23] "Lord, if you had been here my brother would not have died." Yet there was a tender shoot of God-graced confidence hidden underneath her mantle of control and she continued, "but even now I know that whatever you ask from God, God will give you." Jesus told her that her brother would rise, and Martha, the good Jewish woman, nodded her intellectual assent. "I know that he will rise again at the resurrection on the last day."

Resurrection, however, is not an event. Resurrection is a person. And, at this moment, he is looking her straight in the eye.

"Martha, I am the resurrection and the life…Do you believe this?" And in this moment she was relieved of her control and filled with deep spiritual insight. "Yes, Lord, I believe that you are the Christ, the Son of God, who is coming into the world." Martha's words in this moment mark the clearest confession of Jesus' identity in the entire Gospel of John. Hers was the confession of the Apostle Peter, the confession to which the Lord replied,

> Blessed are you, Simon Bar-Jonah! For flesh and blood has not revealed this to you, but my Father who is in heaven. And I tell you, you are Peter, and on this rock I will build my church, and the gates of hell shall not prevail against it.[24]

In this moment Martha becomes a witness filled with faith in the resurrection power of Jesus himself.

Unfortunately, familiar patterns are as comfortable as a pair of old shoes. A few verses later Jesus commanded them to remove the stone, and Martha informed him that the body would have "an odor" after four days. So Jesus lifted the control from her soul again. "Did I not tell you that if you believed you would see the glory of God?"

After Martha's brother was raised from the dead this family gave a dinner in Jesus' honor.[25] This was neither the time nor the venue for a celebratory event. The atmosphere was tense. Raising Lazarus was the miracle that hardened the Pharisees' decision to put Jesus to death. Death warrants were, in fact, being issued— eventually for Lazarus as well as Jesus. We are told that, from this point on, Jesus "no longer walked freely among the Jews."[26]

But because Martha had been released from her imprisoning control, she moved with an extraordinary confidence. Such confidence comes only to those who keep their eyes fixed on Jesus and not on their circumstances. And "Martha served."

Mary

I love personal retreats. I love the quiet. I love the time to hear and speak to the Father, interact with Jesus as he walks with me and be filled again with the Holy Spirit's graces. But for many years I didn't want to return to everyday life. I liked these retreats as a place to escape to, not a place to proceed from. I loved being with Jesus, I just wasn't quite so enamored with coming home.

I think Martha's sister, Mary, was a kindred spirit in this regard. Her heart, like mine, was hungry. She wanted nothing except to sit at Jesus' feet and listen to him. She is a lovely picture of awakening receptivity to God—focused and perhaps a bit naïve. From the very beginning, her desires and actions came under attack—beginning with her sister's protest. And in this first encounter, Jesus simply stepped in and shielded Mary. "Martha, Martha, you are anxious and troubled about many things. Mary has chosen the good portion, which will not be taken away from her."[27]

In retrospect, we know that "the good portion" for Mary was to listen to Jesus—that open-hearted, willing-to-be-changed-by-what-she-heard receptivity. But I wonder if Mary initially thought the good portion was to sit with Jesus. Could it be that this Mary, like I, began her journey inhibited by a bit of passivity? Sitting is generally safer and far more comfortable than moving.

But real life always intervenes. And then what is to be done? Even when Lazarus had died and it appeared that all tangible hope was gone, Mary characteristically remained seated in the house while Martha rushed out to meet Jesus when he finally arrived. Did she think he would eventually come in and find her? That's what he had done before. Didn't he always work the same way? Of course, she might have been so paralyzed in her grief she didn't believe she could possibly move. In any event, Jesus didn't come into the house this time. Instead, he called her to come out to him. If she was caught in any passivity, she was not permitted to stay confined in it. Rather, she responded immediately, rising to meet him where he was and saying the same thing to Jesus that Martha said, "Lord, if you had been here my brother would not have died." And while Jesus had once stepped in and shielded her from any potential pain, this time he stepped fully into the pain with her.

The Scriptures tell us that Jesus wept. But this was no mere teary-eyed sympathy for a friend's grief. The Greek word for "wept" is a strong word, an angry, painful, confrontational word, a word that reveals Jesus' deep outrage with the evil that had precipitated Lazarus' death and prompted Mary's grief. Jesus not only entered into her pain, he went underneath it, on all sides of it, stared it down, and, in the end, lifted the very cause of her grief from her aching heart. And in this preemptive strike over death he not only raised Lazarus from the dead, but drew out the remaining shards of passivity from Mary's heart even as he had simultaneously removed the mantel of compulsive control from Martha's shoulders.

How do we know? When we last see her in John 12, we observe a Mary who had tasted Jesus' protection both as the one who had stepped in and shielded her, and the one who had entered so fully into her pain that he had first carried it with her and then lifted it off of her. And now, in the midst of all the chaos surrounding Jesus' impending death, her confidence in him provided the foundation for the singular moment on Jesus' road to the cross when a human being actually got it right.

The context wasn't at all "safe" from any human perspective. Mary walked into a room full of tense men who were reclining at table with one eye on the door. They knew that the Pharisees were looking for them. This was not a moment conducive to an extravagant, unpredictable action on the part of one of the women of the household. Nevertheless we find Mary again at Jesus' feet, but this time she has exchanged any former passivity for a robe of protected purpose that has permeated every fiber. She knelt and quietly anointed Jesus' feet with extravagant ointment. And the most uptight man in the room led the ensuing attack.

I wonder if Mary knew why she was doing such a thing. I suspect that if we were to have asked her, we would have received an answer similar to the instructions given to the two disciples who would soon be sent to untie a young colt for Jesus to ride into Jerusalem: "The Lord has need of it."[28]

But in that moment any explanation she might have offered was irrelevant. The Lord completely wrapped her up in his protection. He firmly stepped in: "Leave her alone." He supplied the rational explanation she may or may not have had—"She needs to keep it for the day of my burial." And he guided her next steps—Hold onto the ointment, Mary. You will soon need it for more than my feet.

This Mary traveled the long road from a young woman who began the journey by listening in the safety of her home to the one who could freely act in the midst of opposition and fear. But the farther she traveled, the safer she knew herself to be. She could shed her passivity because she knew that as long as her confidence was in Jesus, she did not need to be afraid.

In order to be faithful to the text and to life, we cannot miss the first act in this mighty story of healing. For, while Lazarus is raised from the dead, and Martha and Mary are each met in their individual pain and need, Jesus failed to meet their estimated time of arrival.

> Now Jesus loved Martha and her sister and Lazarus. So, when he heard that Lazarus was ill, he stayed two days longer in the place where he was.[29]

Two days longer! I recognize this Jesus. He doesn't come when we bid him. He comes in his own time, in his own way, for his own purposes.

During my early twenties I began to pray a prayer that simply became the "want to want" prayer. One summer, while working at a Bible camp, I had received a brief, sweet taste of living in the presence of the Lord. I was filled with a kind of peace and joy that I had never experienced before. And the more I tasted, the hungrier I grew. Psalm 63 marked that twentieth summer of my life: "My soul thirsts for you; my flesh faints for you, as in a dry and weary land where there is no water."

But then I returned to college, met my future husband, graduated and began an "adult" life, and my spiritual taste buds grew dull. I began to pray the "want to want" prayer. "Lord, I want to want to know you." I'm afraid the following reality may not be particularly encouraging. I prayed that prayer, in one form or another, for fifteen years. No amount of quiet times, spiritual retreats, or service projects could secure the answer to this cry of my heart. But I could long for what I did not yet taste. And when, in his good pleasure, the timing was right, my heart was ready.

Two days. Fifteen years. It's Jesus' call. But he sees and knows us as fully in his apparent absence as in his palpable presence, and when he moves, it is always for the glory of his Father, which might just include the joy of our own awakening confidence in him.

Sisters

There are several women in this room with me as I write. Our mentor Mary, a forgiven prostitute, and two first-century sisters join me here. But so does one other woman. She is the first woman to name God as "the God who sees." Her name is Hagar. When Sarai gets weary of waiting for a child, she decides to take the birthing of Abram's heir into her own hands and, in the custom of the day, offers her husband the womb of her servant. After Hagar becomes pregnant the relationship between the two women rapidly degenerates. Sarai "dealt with her harshly, and she fled."[30] But an angel of the Lord finds her in the desert and promises her a life and a future. And as her soul is healed, she calls on the name of the Lord by addressing him as "the God who sees...truly here I have seen him who looks after me."[31]

I wonder if Mary, Jesus' mother, ever thought about Hagar during the moments when it appeared that her son did not see her. As a singular mother she was called to share her son in a singular way. While it was her son's vocation to reach out to many women—seeing them, befriending them, healing them—his mother stood shadowed behind a sword aimed right at her heart. Yet she must have carried a grace-filled confidence in "the God who sees" within that heart as she walked her own private agony until the moment she finally stood under his cross. And then, with Hagar, she was able to say in real time what her heart had known by faith, "truly here I have seen him who looks after me."

Hiding But Not Hidden

I was in my living room with a friend who sat scratching my English Springer Spaniel's ears—thus becoming his newest best friend—while she told me of recent events in her life. On Friday her boss had come into her office after work and told her she was terminated. No prior conversation, no explanation other than, "It's not a good fit."

There are many paths that lie in front of a person at such a moment. Anger. Defensiveness. Insistence upon an explanation. But the deep path in my friend's soul immediately took a different road: "Lord, what on earth are you doing? I was comfortable here. I liked the work. I could make a contribution. I felt safe. And suddenly I find myself being sent out the door...what is going on here?" With this deep question simmering just under the surface her response to her boss came in two rapid stages. A most articulate woman, when she was first confronted with the news she told her former boss that she really loved the mission of the organization and certainly respected the need for them to have the appropriate employees. At the same time, she expressed her shock at not understanding why she wasn't a good fit. Gradually, however, the deeper response in her soul came bubbling to the surface and even as she was speaking she began to wonder if, at the bottom of it all, her boss might be on to something. And so she soon found herself saying, "Perhaps it's not a good fit. Give me a hug and I'll pack up my things and go." And, as she told me, "I couldn't wait to get back to my apartment to ask the Lord what on earth he might be up to."

I sat in my recliner, taking it all in with some astonishment. Since that moment she had, of course, been given lots of counsel: "Fight it. Defend your rights. Don't lose your anger." But I found my spirit soaring. For one thing, I told her, it is much better to be terminated without a good reason than to suffer a few more months while an organization manufactures one. A simple "go" can be an extraordinary act of grace on the Lord's part.

But then our conversation took a different turn. The job really wasn't a good fit. It was comfortable and "safe," but, in truth, she was too big for it. She was choosing to squeeze herself into a smaller space than she ought to be filling. She is a strong, educated, gifted woman, and it was almost as though she had been hiding in a place where she could make a contribution without being noticed or stretched...or hurt.

I observed this interesting split in her soul—on the one hand she wanted to be comfortable. That is the self that had settled into "safe" employment. On the other hand, she was ready for life to be an adventure. That is the self that hugged the director and, at some level, skipped home to find out what the Lord might be up to.

And she responded, "Oh, Carla, I know what this issue is. I don't want to be hurt again. I have already been in one situation where I gave everything I had, was everything I am, and I was so beat up. It took me years to get rid of the pain. I don't want to go there again."

How well I understood my friend. After her heart had been pierced by a few poisonous arrows, she wanted to run and hide. She wanted to protect herself because it hurt so badly to be attacked at such a fundamental level, and hiding is the only safety she knew.

My friends in the New Testament have, thus far, faced many struggles, including loneliness, disappointment, fear and sin. Jesus' decisive action met each woman's real need. But the story of the friend in my living room sets another issue squarely before us. There is no real receptivity without her close companion, vulnerability.[32] It has always been so. The Psalms are full of the pain and the glory of this reality:

For God alone, O my soul,

wait in silence,

For my hope is from him.

He only is my rock and my salvation,

My fortress; I shall not be shaken.[33]

But how do we move from confidence in God as a lovely sentiment of biblical poetry to an existential reality when such vulnerability tops the list of our fears?

The very nature of receptivity brings with it an intense desire to know that we are going to be safe if and when we open our soul's gate to another. Sometimes, of course, we can mistake mere discomfort for lack of safety. For example, wise exhortation and correction are rarely pleasant at the time they are offered but that does not, by definition, render the situation unsafe. When our hearts are receptive to God's truth we can value the wisdom of others, even as it is imperfectly offered. Clear conviction can come from the Lord through all-too-human human instruments. We will know the signature of such wise counsel by its clarity. We will know how to respond to what we hear.

But when we have opened the gate of our soul and experience our encounters with others as attacks or condemnation, any potential grain of truth that may have been spoken comes coated with a paralyzing poison that pierces a receptive heart with confusion and fear. These experiences are very painful, and when they occur our instinctive response is to hide.

To be human is to be vulnerable. Vulnerability is both the glory and the agony of a receptive heart, open to the spontaneity of real life and, in consequence, to the risks of real pain. Yet human vulnerability is the only human soil in which confidence in God can be firmly rooted and grow strong within us.

Self-Protection

Our instinctual response to vulnerability, however, is self-protection. Receptivity's gate clangs shut. The bolt is swiftly slid into place. Self-protection obstructs any real opportunity to discover how God truly heals and protects his people. When we self-protect we find ourselves hunkering down behind inanimate objects of our own making. At times we find that we have forged self-protective armor—link by link. Or perhaps we have, instead, woven a cloak of invisibility—thread upon thread. Either way, we are caught in self-protection's tyrannical trap and cannot reach the bolt of receptivity's gate. For if we would be healed, we must first be found.

Self-Forged Armor

Several years ago I was going through a challenging time when I felt deeply betrayed by a trusted friend. I was angry. I was not only angry at him, I was angry at every male on the planet, including my husband, although he personally had done nothing to merit my anger. But at that moment my heart was painting all men with the same brush. One night, when Wyatt innocently reached over to take an uneaten slice of apple off my plate as we finished dinner, I stabbed his hand with my fork. Fortunately, I did not hurt him, but I was frightened at the strength of my anger, for I knew that if I did not take on the real battle of forgiving my friend, I was in serious danger of forging my own suit of armor.

Self-protective armor can be forged by our anger whether the links are hot, bitter and defensive or cold, icy and withdrawn. Rather than fleeing to the cross of Christ with our pain, we nurse it, and, in failing to fight the battle of releasing the offending party to Jesus and living hidden within the spaciousness of Christ's righteousness, we build up our own defenses. Sometimes we attack our offender, sometimes we simply choose not to care anymore. Either choice encases us in rigid self-protection that hardens our hearts. When we wear such armor, "don't mess with me" is the message that arrives before we even enter a room. So no one messes with us—or knows us, either. As one of my friends recently observed while processing her self-protective responses to a difficult situation, "I was so hurt that I withdrew to protect myself. What I didn't realize was that I had created a wall so high that those who would encourage and love me were as shut out as those who had hurt me."

Cold competence can be another form of carefully forged armor. We can be really good at what we do, but rather than rejoicing that the Lord could have good use of us, our goal is to do this one thing better than anyone we know. So competition replaces cooperation, climbing to the top is more important than helping someone else find their own next step, and results become more important than the process by which they are achieved. We are well defended—but our inevitable coldness pierces those around us with life-numbing ice rather than flooding them with life-giving warmth.

And finally, we can forge armor by becoming super-rational. This is a particular trap for anyone whose natural gifting comes in an intellectual package. Analytic thought can become a specialized shield. We can live from the neck up, never feeling the pain in our hearts because we are not in touch with anything we cannot analyze. I well remember the frank young woman who neatly summed up my mid-twenties with the following observation—"Carla, sometimes you come across like a ton of bricks." This observation of my forceful defenses was only reinforced when, during that same period of time, my own perceptive mother helpfully observed that perhaps it would be best if I explored a career that did not put me in direct contact with people.

Super-rational interactions with others can also become a weapon. My husband will occasionally hold up the mirror to my face and show me my intellectual armor when I refuse to hear the intent of his words and coldly analyze the verbiage he is using instead. I am tempted to reach for my coat of mail whenever he has touched a place in me that is so sore that no self-protection but mental metal will suffice.

The trouble with armor is that it works. An encased heart is protected. But we wear such armor at tremendous cost. It is heavy and confining. After awhile our hearts themselves grow hard. We relinquish the capacity to be known and to know, to be loved and to love, because we have become so adept at locking others out.

I wonder if the Samaritan woman's jar was not, in part, a symbol of her armor.[34] The fourth chapter of John's Gospel never tells us the details of why the woman at the well had been wed to five different men and was now living with a sixth. The popular assumption is that she was a prostitute. But we have no evidence to that effect. She might have been barren and handed from one man to another—marked as one who could not give her husband children. She might simply have been quite difficult to live with——or had the inexplicable knack of being attracted to men who were difficult to live with. Perhaps there was a different story attached to the ending of each relationship. Whatever the details of her life were we know two things for sure: she was not married to the man she was currently living with and she was isolated from the women of her community. No one living in the desert voluntarily shows up at high noon to draw water.

But weary as he was on this hot day, Jesus approached her— and was promptly confronted by her protective armor. She immediately began to hide her hurting heart behind questions—good questions, but nevertheless guarded ones. Jesus, why are you breaking all of our cultural rules to talk to me? Where are you getting this water you talk about? Besides, you don't have anything to draw water with. Who do you think you are? Yet, in response to Jesus' patient invitation, she removed her intellectual armor for just a moment and we glimpse the thirsty longing of a woman who asked to drink from his cup in place of the one she had, at his request, just shared with him.

But then round two began. When Jesus brought up the subject of her husbands she quickly donned her armor and headed down a much safer mental path. Where are we supposed to be worshiping? Who is right, the Samaritans or the Jews? Here was a woman who was quite adept at deflecting the pain in her heart by engaging in analytic conversations. It was a great question and theologians have pondered Jesus' ensuing response ever since. But it was also a question more than likely intended to distract from the personal issue at hand.

In the end, Jesus told her that he was the Christ. This overwhelming revelation completely disarmed her. She left her jar—and, with it, her armor—at the well and went back to her village undefended and desirous of transparent communication with the very people from whom she had been protecting herself. "Come and see a man who told me all that I ever did." And then she asked the only real question of the day, the question that had already begun to liberate her from her self-protective armor—"Can this be the Christ?"

A Cloak of Invisibility

Perhaps we don't forge armor well. Or perhaps we have become too weary to engage the world around us at all. It may just be easier to become invisible. Invisibility is a humanly understandable way to self-protect when we experience ourselves as ignored or erased by others. Our thoughts, words or actions go unacknowledged. We begin to believe the lie that whatever we have been given to offer the world might as well not exist because it goes unperceived by those persons whose recognition matters most to us.

When we are consistently ignored we often experience ourselves as mute—having nothing of value to say, because it appears to us that no one—or least the one that matters—is listening to us. Being ignored or marginalized is a subversive attack against all the good seed that has been planted within us, all that is in the vulnerable stages of growth, all that is already in bloom. And when we are not seen as growing beings, our hearts can begin to shrivel up. After awhile invisibility becomes so familiar that we voluntarily reach out for this enfeebling cloak. It just seems normal.

Preferring a cloak of invisibility was the plight of a certain woman who heard that Jesus was in town.[35] If ever there was a woman who understood what it meant to be marginalized and erased, it would be this woman in Luke 8. She was physically ill. She must have been very weak—twelve years of bleeding without ceasing would have rendered her terribly anemic in addition to whatever other pain had plagued her with such persistence. She would have been unable to bear children, and there is no husband in evidence. She was poor, having spent all she had on physicians who had not only failed to help her, but, in fact, had only made her suffering worse. Furthermore, the particular nature of her ailment made her unfit to be found in any social context. "If a woman has a discharge of blood for many days, not at the time of her menstrual period...all the days of the discharge she shall continue in uncleanness."[36] Invisibility had become a familiar old cloak after so many years of physical, emotional, and social pain.

But she had heard the reports about Jesus. And the common theme in all of them was Jesus' healing engagement with others wearing a similar cloak of marginalization by society—he had cleansed a leper,[37] raised up a paralytic,[38] and straightened out a man's withered hand.[39] Jesus had even permitted a prostitute to touch him with an unparalleled intimacy that was, at one and the same time, completely safe and utterly holy.[40]

And so, when she heard that Jesus was near, she found herself in the crowd. Not just on the edge, where the combined force of her body's weakness, her soul's woundedness and her society's boundaries should have kept her confined. Her cloak of invisibility served her well as she crept closer and closer—until she was right behind him. Perhaps Jesus' reported words to that other woman echoed in her soul: "your faith has saved you, go in peace, your faith has saved you..."[41] What we do know is that she told herself, "If only I touch his garment I will be made well." Deliberately attempting to draw no attention to herself she desperately reached out and touched him. And her body was instantly healed.

But before she could escape as invisibly as she had come, everything around her came to a halt. And she heard, above her head, a terrifying question—"Who was it that touched me?" Like an animal sensing its danger, she froze, quivering with fear as she waited for the moment to pass. With relief she heard the disciples dismiss Jesus' question—he was being carried along in a crowd that was pressing in from every side. Everyone was touching him. But Jesus would not move. "Someone has touched me, for I perceive that power has gone from me."

> And when the woman saw that she was not hidden, she came trembling, and falling down before him declared in the presence of all the people why she had touched him, and how she had been immediately healed.[42]

She who was so used to being invisible was suddenly both seen and heard. She had known enough about Jesus to come, but not enough to anticipate how profoundly he would know her need. It was not only this woman's body that needed restoration. Her very existence in this world needed radical affirmation. She had long ago dissociated from her need to be known and loved. But Jesus knew. And so, falling at his feet she told him—and anyone within hearing distance—her story. And raising her to her feet, her old cloak of invisibility was fully and finally lifted off of her as he looked her in the eye and, blessing her, said, "Daughter, your faith has made you well; go in peace."[43]

Friend. Woman. Daughter. The stories of Jesus' tender healing of these women must surely have reached his mother's ears. In these moments, did Mary ponder the wise words of her own song? Jesus was indeed exalting those of humble estate. Did she remember Simeon's words of the rising of many in Israel? These women were most certainly being raised up from their marginalized state. Would not her confidence in God's gracious protection of the vulnerable have been strengthened as she listened and held the stories of these healings close to the place she had once held her child? In the midst of it all, she kept her vulnerable vigil and waited for the healing of her own hurting heart.

Jesus' Touch

The word of God is, indeed, so potent that "no one suffers from being remote in time or place...We find always the same perfect immediacy of communication that was given to those [Jesus] met on the roads of Palestine."[44] Over the course of a lifetime, we may discover ourselves identifying with all of these women: the forgiven sinner at Simon's house; Martha, whose genuine competence was purged of inappropriate control; her sister, Mary, who greatly preferred sitting comfortably with Jesus than moving in any intentional manner; the Samaritan woman who hid her aching loneliness behind the armor of her functional jug; the bleeding woman the doctors could not heal and her neighbors would not touch.

I have often pondered why the stories of Jesus' interactions with women are related in so much vivid detail. I wonder if the healing of these women does not open all of our hearts to receive a particular protective grace of our God. I am so grateful that they are written this way, for these sisters in the communion of saints help us, men and women alike, to touch the hem of our Savior's robe.

But the reaching is not first ours. Jesus, knowing that we, like these women, would need to know his tangible presence, established a way to touch all men and women of all time. He accomplished it by means of a meal. In his hands, bread and wine have become the one sure place where "I am with you always"[45] can truly be tasted. As we lift up our hands to receive Communion's simple gifts, we find that the hands that first broke that bread are now stretched out to us at the point of our need.

As C.S. Lewis once said of this holy meal, "here a hand from a hidden country touches not only my soul, but my body."[46]

Every so often I meet one of the women Jesus first touched as I kneel at the communion rail. Sometimes I find her right next to me. Sometimes she's resting just behind the friend I had coffee with last week whose need for Jesus' touch is so much like her own. More often I meet my first-century friends at a much-needed point during a given week and carry them in my heart the next time I share in the Lord's Supper.

And in these timeless moments I am reminded that I have been drawn into a common story with the same Jesus, and have the same needs that wait for the same touch of the same hand. I would like to say the only difference between my first-century friends and me is that I have to walk by faith, but upon reflection, even that isn't very different.

So, carrying in my own heart the same song of confidence set into the heart of a transparent Samaritan woman and a woman who is no longer invisible, I offer this response to the young woman who sat in my living room petting my dog, knowing she had been choosing to hide so that she would not be hurt again.

"Dear friend, there is a great difference between hiding and being hidden. Let go of your armor. Do not stand at the edge of the crowd. Look—He finds you behind your jar. Touch—He will restore far more than you can ask for."

And then I hear Jesus' mother joining the song. Do not be afraid—a sword can pierce the heart, but it will never destroy those who put their faith in God. Has he not said, "Your faith has saved you?" Go in peace—you whom he calls his daughters, you whom he makes his friends.

Buoyancy

On the third day there was a wedding at Cana in Galilee, and the mother of Jesus was there. Jesus also was invited to the wedding with his disciples. When the wine ran out, the mother of Jesus said to him, "They have no wine." And Jesus said to her, "Woman, what does this have to do with me? My hour has not yet come." His mother said to the servants, "Do whatever he tells you."

Now there were six stone water jars there for the Jewish rites of purification, each holding twenty or thirty gallons. Jesus said to the servants, "Fill the jars with water." And they filled them up to the brim. And he said to them, "Now draw some out and take it to the master of the feast." So they took it. When the master of the feast tasted the water now become wine, and did not know where it came from (though the servants who had drawn the water knew), the master of the feast called the bridegroom and said to him, "Everyone serves the good wine first, and when people have drunk freely, then the poor wine. But you have kept the good wine until now." This, the first of his signs, Jesus did at Cana in Galilee, and manifested his glory. And his disciples believed in him. (John 2:1-11)

"Do Whatever He Tells You"

By this time, Mary's receptive heart was deeply formed. She had found that the Lord was indeed merciful, making his home with her in her own humble estate and filling her hungry soul with good things, perhaps especially in the achingly difficult moments when the shadow of the ever-present sword had momentarily obscured her vision. In those moments, though perplexed, she could only ponder and wait. But this much she knew for certain—the heart of the God she knew beat in the heart of her son.

Jesus had left home for a time and then returned to Nazareth with a few new friends. Mary, Jesus and his new disciples were all invited to the nearby town of Cana for a wedding celebration. Since the women's quarters were normally close to where the wine was stored it was perhaps not surprising that Mary first heard of the family's serious hospitality crisis. The wedding would run for seven days, and it would have been unthinkable that the wine would not keep pace. At the very least it would have been the kind of social embarrassment to the family that neighbors would have jested about for years. "Remember their wedding? Can you believe they ran out of wine?" Perhaps they lacked the means to provide the quantity needed for such an event. Perhaps more people came than they anticipated. Perhaps robbers had hijacked the supply of wine they ordered. In any event, Mary gathered up the family distress into her heart and carried it for a moment as though it was her own. And then she laid the need at the feet of her son.

But Jesus had entered into a new phase of life. He had submitted to his mother and foster father in Nazareth for a long season. But everything was changing. The mother who had once borne this son in the ark of her own womb was, in her own way, in the process of releasing him onto the dry ground that was his alone. Now Jesus had been baptized in water and a dove had rested on him as it had once flown to Noah; only this time the dove bore the blessing of his Father instead of a simple olive leaf. And the dove hadn't flown away. It had rested and remained on Jesus. Something absolutely unique was afoot.

So when her oblique statement, "they have no more wine," was met with her son's respectful, yet firm, "Woman, what does this have to do with me? My hour has not yet come," Mary must have felt the waves crashing over her head. This independent son was not the submissive young man she had raised. He was so focused, so final. She could not have known then what was only clear after his passion—that the "hour" signified his long road to the cross. Had she known, she may have been tempted to retract the veiled request on behalf of her friends. But Jesus was out of her motherly reach, and her life would never be the same again. The ark that had once borne him must have experienced a momentary shudder.

But just as the crashing waves and unstable seas had not destroyed the vessel carrying Noah and his family, neither did they destroy Mary. Like a buoyant little ark of the Lord, she bounded back to the surface and swiftly grasped the deep bearings of her faith. With courage and cheerfulness of soul, Mary turned to the servants and said, "Do whatever he tells you." And the one righteous man took over.

The Wind in Our Sails

The "Feminine" Ship

Time stops for me in a little vacation town on the eastern side of Lake Michigan. For all the years of my childhood and well into my twenties, my family would take a couple of weeks every summer and go to the "big" lake. There we would play in the fine white sand, jump in the waves and walk the long, unobstructed beach. As we grew older, my sisters and I would sing every verse of every hymn we knew as we walked together up and down that beloved beach.

But my most vivid memory of life on Lake Michigan occurred when I was about eight years old. I was puttering about the shore on a breezy day, watching my uncle and father attempt to learn how to sail. I became absolutely riveted on the mast of their new little sailboat as the unpredictable wind would catch the sail for a few breath-taking moments, only capriciously to twitch them into a plummeting nosedive into the lake. My uncle and father would come bobbing to the surface, right their small craft and board her again. Then I would see the wind snap the sail, and the boat would travel a little farther up the coast. A few moments later the boat would capsize. All this time the current was carrying them farther up shore, so this diverting spectacle became increasingly less detailed and, therefore, more pronounced. I watched in deliciously horrified fascination for hours, awed by this brave little boat's ability to continue to right herself as she persistently tutored the two brothers.

Once my father got his bearings I spent many delightful moments on that little sailboat. Here I first experienced the fullness of silence that is only broken by the rhythmic ripple of waves and heard the response of trees when the leaves catch the whispers of wind. On that little craft I learned to shift my place by bending low, responding to what the water, the wind and the waves were doing. While I would have no words for the experience for decades, it was the first dawning in my awareness of something "other" that was, in her own right, feminine.

How is a ship "feminine" in the manner I have been contemplating in this book? I had always thought of a ship as "she" because she was "home" away from home. Ships throughout the centuries have borne names and mast-heads that would certainly suggest this possibility. Christopher Columbus made his long journey on the *Niña, Pinta* and *Santa Maria.* The Pilgrims, in hope of again seeing spring on another shore, embarked upon the *Mayflower.* But the feminine contours of reality embedded in a ship are distinctly different from a woman's womb, the fertile earth or responsive souls. The ship is not alive. There can be no germination, no pregnancy, no promise of fruit. A ship will bear but it will never give birth.

And yet, there are two fundamental properties of a ship that offer a fitting conclusion to this extended meditation on the relationship of creaturely response to divine initiative. The task of a ship is to navigate through calm days and stormy nights to carry treasure to its desired destination. In order to arrive safely home, receptive sails must catch unpredictable winds and tenacious hulls must weather innumerable storms. And in the nexus between wind and sail, between storm and hull, we discover two more facets of God's grace as we are piloted into ports, as we are healed and held.

The very sails of a ship were designed to be profoundly receptive to the wind's slightest waft and strongest gale. At the peak of their prominence at sea, the "square-rigged sails" of the large clipper ships were designed for incredible speed and agility. But they were at the mercy of the wind and were in most serious straits where there was none.

> Calms and doldrums were always a greater curse to the square-rigger than any storm. She could fight the gale up to full storm strength, but she could only roll, sweat and wallow in the useless calm. And auxiliary power was ruin, not answer.[1]

If the ship was to come safely into harbor, her well-formed sails had first to receive the wind that came to her and then channel it to good purpose. Formed, waiting and ready, she was nothing without an elemental wind in her sails.

So, while a good sailor was trained to catch the wind once it presented itself, he knew he could not create that wind. This reality required dependence upon a force outside the sailor's own power. The sailor's awareness of the fundamental vulnerability of a comparatively small vessel in a large ocean has occasioned countless hymns and prayers for safety at sea. The sailors and their loved ones could not place their confidence in skill alone; not only were there mysterious perils in the great deeps, but even the shallow shoals hid reefs and rocks with biting teeth that broke up crafts even as the safety of land lay just beyond her reach. The sailors were truly at the mercy of a wind they could not manufacture.

But the ship's sails, like artificial wings, would fly ineffectually across the water unless they were attached to a hull. As in all things "feminine," the hull is the body of the boat, intended to protect a treasure that another has deposited deep within her hold until she reaches her appointed destination. No doubt, the ship's hold could be horribly misused, as when human beings were transported as cargo to be bought and sold. But the abuse of the ship's interior only accentuates the purpose for which she is truly intended—a ship is crafted to carry treasure in her hold from the time she embarks on her journey until she arrives at her designated port of call. The bulk of the ship's hull lies under the water hidden from view and cradles the precious contents in her hold for as long as the task is required of her. The treasure doesn't change as it is carried from one port to another. But the hull can change a great deal. She can suffer serious injury if a sharp object along the way gouges her. And with waves constantly beating against her sides, she can surely grow thin in places from time to time.

As the conveyor of all that is precious, the hull has one fundamental virtue. She has to be buoyant. Not only must she herself remain afloat; her task is to keep the treasure within her afloat as well. This charge is most delightful on idyllic days when the sea is enveloped in a rising breeze. On such days the drag of the wind on the surface of the water merely causes ripples to form as that ship glides effortlessly through them. And there is also the exhilarating joy of the hale and hearty days where a well-fitted ship can cover great expanses of sea as she bounds over the waves before her.

But there are the other days as well, moments when the skies darken and the hatches above the hull are battened down with tarpaulins to protect the treasure secured within her hold. During these times the ship rocks with howling winds, crashing waves and water coming down from above as well as up from below. And in these moments the ship's buoyancy becomes her lifeline. If she can rebound under such stress the mast timbers might crack and even fall, yet all is not lost. But if her weather-beaten belly springs leaks or is gouged by sharp objects from below and her buoyancy is stripped from her, the ship will sink.

I freely admit that one will not find the word "buoyancy" in any biblical list of human responses to God's multi-faceted grace, but that does not mean she is not present. The Scriptures have a great deal to say about endurance and patience, and these surely share some vital characteristics with the qualities of our sister ship. Josef Pieper describes endurance as "a strong activity of the soul, namely, a vigorous grasping and clinging to the good." One can see the whole ship braced for the next gust of wind and crash of wave. Similarly, patience comprises the capacity to "preserve cheerfulness and serenity of mind in spite of injuries suffered in the realization of the good."[2] There is a rebounding quality to buoyancy. The ship has signed on for adventure and she will take her knocks as they come. Endurance and patience are not "active" qualities in the sense of charting passages or navigating toward destinations. They are, rather, the "receptive" facets of courage formed in us as we learn to move forward in quiet intentionality.

When these firm responses to God's grace are present, storms are weathered and crises overcome. Our ultimate port of call is certain, even if the path we take is not the route we originally envisioned. But without such attentiveness to the rolling deck under our feet we run the risk of passing through life without ever having lived in wise, grounded response to any real moment of it. Rather, we placate ourselves with the soul-deadening monotony of retracing the past and mapping out a future over which we have very limited control.

Buoyancy is feminine because of the inherent spiritual architecture formed in the bearer to carry this facet of God's sustaining grace. Here a buoyant human response joins the chorus of all created things in touch with their dependence as they sing out, "Lord, unless you accomplish your work in me, it will not be done." This particular response names suffering and weakness for the existential realities they really are and then lives within the simple, receptive posture of one who, having placed her confidence in God, is enabled to carry his gifts within her hold. In so doing, even though she may greatly suffer, she will not sink.

The most achingly beautiful picture of feminine buoyancy I have witnessed is one young widow's determination to live honestly and record transparently the storm that wracked her young family during the last year of her brave husband's recurrent battle with cancer. Reading her blog through those final months was an experience in laughter and tears in a single breath, riding breaker upon breaker of absorbed shocks and rebounding courage. With the strong arms of family, community and her God around her she made home for her young children and simultaneously rode out the waves alongside her husband until he reached his ultimate destination. Receiving the particular grace she needed for her extraordinary need, this grieving woman has become one of the most buoyant vessels I have ever known.

While our circumstances differ, all finite human beings inevitably come to places in life where our illusions of control are stripped away and our carefully laid plans lay tattered at our feet. In those moments only God's breath filling our sails and his strong hands holding our hull together will guide our ship and all that is within her safely into port. But if we would rise to life's worst storms, the formation will not begin in the gale, but in the small puddles that splash at our feet when no one is looking.

So what is spiritual buoyancy? Buoyancy is the moment-by-moment adjustment of a fragile vessel renewed and propelled by God's abounding grace. It is the sensitive response of God's people to the wind-that-blows-where-it-wills.

At a time when sailing vessels were more central to human experience than they are today, our mentor Mary was described in nautical terms—consider this stanza of a sixth century hymn reflecting on Mary's part in redemption's plan: "ship which bore treasure and blessings from the house of the Father and came and poured out riches on our destitute earth."[3] Just as Mary has been understood as the ark bearing Jesus, so the church is, by extension, the ark that still bears Jesus—carrying his life and his people within her hold. St. Cyprian's famous declaration comes to mind:

> He can no longer have God for his Father, who
> has not the Church for his mother. If any one
> could escape who was outside the ark of Noah,
> then he also may escape who shall be outside of
> the Church.[4]

There is no true "I" in the kingdom of God without an accompanying "we." We will never navigate life's storms by ourselves. My own congregation was blessed by our forebears with a traditionally vivid reminder of the church as the sanctuary for Noah, his family—and for us. When I look up from my pew I see an inverted ark above my head. I am reminded that every Christian is carried within her hull.

The Current and Wind of the Spirit

In this final chapter I want first to consider the relationship between two feminine realities in the kingdom of God and the Holy Spirit's work within them. Jesus has secured passage on the ark of the church for every baptized Christian. At the same time, to be human is to be a unique vessel, complete with sail and hull of our own. The Holy Spirit propels both ark and small craft in a manner that converges for the welfare of both. For, just as current and wind are both required if sailing vessels are to make their way across mighty oceans, the Holy Spirit also moves uniquely within and between these respective spiritual ships.

Like the Gulf Stream—that strong, predictable movement of ocean currents caused by wind, the impact of continents and the earth's rotation[5]—the pastoral office is the strong, predictable movement of the Spirit. Here fundamental gifts like the preaching of the word, baptism and communion are stewarded for the good of each person within the ark. A second movement of the Spirit, the mysterious wind-that-blows-where-it-wills, [6] complements this strong current. This wind catches unique sails by means of the graces, or *charisms,* of the Spirit, given, as God wills, to individual members of the body for the good of the whole.[7] When predictable currents and the wind-that-blows-where-it-wills converge, the church is blessed and the ark both protects the people within and responds to the new things God is delighting to do as he blows fresh winds across her bow.

The predictable movement of the Spirit is absolutely essential to the church's stability. Just as captains once determined "trade routes" based on steady ocean currents, ordained church leaders are responsible for administering sacred actions that are both theologically informed and regularly performed. Without baptism we are not "brought safely through water," and the door into the ark remains closed to us.[8] Without the careful proclamation of God's revealed word, wisdom could easily lose her bearings, since she only thrives when that which is received from above is navigable truth. Without the Lord's Supper, the family in this ark would be greatly impoverished, lacking the sustaining experience of being drawn anew into God's great love and being strengthened in our love for each other.

But when stable currents are left without the movement of an infinitely creative wind, any local church, like a particular ship, can find herself in great distress. The demise of the *Dreadnought* vividly illustrates the tragedy of a ship held in the vice of a strong current without the assistance a responsive wind:

> In 1869 the old ship left New York under Captain Mayhew, bound once more to San Francisco. But she never arrived. Whilst making for the Straits of Le Maire, Captain Mayhew got close in under the rock-bound coast of Tierra del Fuego. A heavy swell was running, and the ship was just forging ahead under all sail to her main skysail when it fell calm. Though the *Dreadnought* rolled until the sails threatened to flog themselves to tatters there was nothing to be done. Then it was noticed that a current was carrying the ship towards the land. One can imagine how her crew would employ

every device for bringing up a wind that was known to seamen. The mainmast must have been stuck full of sheath-knives. But it was all in vain. Not a breath stirred aloft. At last, in desperation the boats were lowered, and they tried to tow the ship clear. To tow a fully-loaded 1,400 ton ship in a Cape Horn swell was, of course, an impossibility. As the *Dreadnought* was caught by the breakers, she was hove inshore with irresistible force; then came the crash and all was over—the famous packet soon lay a battered wreck, which the angry surf slowly tore in pieces. Her crew was picked up by a passing ship, after three weeks of suffering, during which they ever had to be on their guard against the hostile Tierra del Fuegians.[9]

If we would avoid the *Dreadnought's* spiritual parallel, strong current alone cannot be the sole driving force in the church. "A Christian life...that consisted only in the sacraments and ministerial functions would soon become repetitive and pure habit."[10] She also needs the life-giving wind-that-blows-where-it-wills in the sails of smaller craft. Without this vibrant, fresh wind of the Spirit, a local congregation, like the *Dreadnought*, can run aground.

There are many ports of call to which Christ's individual vessels are to be sent before we reach our ultimate destination. We are blown to our homes, our communities and, sometimes, to the other side of the world. The wind-that-blows-where-it-wills propels the people of God toward the creative "new thing" God is always delighting to do in, among, and through us. When the creative cargo of God's specific grace for a particular time and place is received, carried and delivered at the Holy Spirit's bidding, we become a responsive people. The spiritual buoyancy formed within us is free to move with the wind wherever it wills to take us.

But such freedom does not leave the current behind. "A Christian life deprived of [the sacraments and ministerial functions], and which consisted only in charismatic spontaneity and innovation, would inevitably end in confusion and the arbitrary use of the will."[11] The combined forces of the current and wind of the Holy Spirit preserve and enliven the other.

A few years ago, I had a lovely experience of the Spirit's stable current and wind-that-blows-where-it-wills working in tandem. I had been invited to give a seminar in Bangkok, Thailand. Once I arrived there, the Thai Christians were prepared to provide for everything I needed. But I had to get there first—and Thailand is literally on the other side of the world from Chicago. My pastor took this project to heart and set the need before a parishioner with more frequent flier miles than I knew were possible to collect. She converted all of those miles into a plane ticket to Bangkok. That gift in itself was extravagant, but there was more. The church gave me an additional monetary gift, provided meals for my husband and son while I was away, and even set cards and candy outside the door of my home on the morning of my departure. I received a gift from others in order to deliver a gift to others. The strong, stable current of my church home lay firmly beneath me, and the Holy Spirit's wind filled my own small sails. The Thai Christians were blessed, I was blessed, and my church was blessed. What delight awaits us when current and wind converge.

Buoyant Freedoms

Our ships, both large ark and small craft, have yet other territory to explore. We have one more guide joining us on this journey— for the Apostle Paul must surely be one of the most buoyant vessels that ever sailed the ocean of life. In his second letter to the Corinthians he writes:

> And God is able to make all grace abound to you,
> so that having all sufficiency in all things at all
> times, you may abound in every good work.[12]

This confident proclamation of the grace of God that fills and even overflows its fragile vessels comes in the midst of a letter full of the transparency of a very human struggle. The Apostle's vision and mission was large, strong and unwavering, but his daily life was a constant adaptation to the rolling surface under his feet.[13] In his exasperated defense of his own ministry against the "super-apostles" who were confusing the church in Corinth, he found himself continually referring to the enormity of the daily struggles in his own life. By this point in his ministry he had been "so utterly burdened" beyond his strength that he had despaired of life itself.[14] But the waves and breakers that crashed over him had not left him shipwrecked. He preferred, rather, to invoke the imagery of a "triumphal procession."[15] Here was a ship with the wind singing through her sails.

"Now the Lord is the Spirit, and where the Spirit of the Lord is there is freedom."[16] How ironic that Paul would most fully celebrate the Spirit's wind of freedom in the very letter where he speaks of the paradoxes in his life. In the second of his three lists of hardships in this letter he tells the church in Corinth:

> We are treated as imposters, and yet are true; as unknown, and yet well known; as dying, and behold, we live; as punished, and yet not killed; as sorrowful, yet always rejoicing; as poor, yet making many rich; as having nothing, yet possessing everything.[17]

An odd description of freedom. But this paradoxical freedom is not unfamiliar to those who would embrace a buoyant Christian life. Whether on halcyon days where nothing could look better or on stormy seas where nothing could look worse, life lived firmly anchored to Christ comes accompanied by a steady sanity that recognizes things are not always as they appear.

Discernment of mere appearances has been a consistent theme throughout these reflections. Some root systems take a long time to grow before anything appears above the ground. Wisdom and folly offer an invitation that differs in tone but not, at first, in words. Confidence in God is the indescribable blessing on the other side of acknowledged vulnerability. Buoyant strength is made perfect in weakness. Spiritual freedom is set in our souls at the pivotal points of paradox.

Two such paradoxical freedoms must surely be numbered among the most vital, yet least celebrated, in our lives. They are the freedom to speak and the freedom to be silent, and her companion, the freedom to be visible and the freedom to be hidden.

I was on retreat with the class whose initial responses propelled me to write this book. They had spent the morning personally pondering Jesus' encounter with the woman at the well, and they returned to our meeting room in a thoughtful silence.

They were quite comfortable with each other by this point, but they didn't want to talk. As I watched them take their places I realized that they would need help to make the transition from wherever they had been with Jesus that morning back to the "normal" conversation of the group.

I told them that they would not be asked to share what they had been pondering, that some things were best left quietly resting for awhile. (This announcement was greeted by an audible sigh of relief.) I then observed that we often speak to fill space, to add to the general noise. We can even give away our most precious secrets, the words gestating within from God, because we think that speech is the default drive and silence is no more than the pauses between words. But that is not the truth about the relationship between silence and holy speech. And I offered them this insight from the Desert Fathers that has long shaped my thoughts on this subject:

> When the door of the steam bath is continually left open, the heat inside rapidly escapes through it; likewise the soul, in its desire to say many things, dissipates its remembrance of God through the door of speech, even though everything it says may be good. Thereafter the intellect, though lacking appropriate ideas, pours out a welter of confused thoughts to anyone it meets, as it no longer has the Holy Spirit to keep its understanding free from fantasy. Ideas of value always shun verbosity, being foreign to confusion and fantasy. Timely silence, then, is precious, for it is nothing less than the mother of the wisest thoughts.[18]

To be free to be silent is one of the deepest feminine freedoms. "Do whatever he tells you" is the last recorded word we ever hear Mary speak.

Silence is intimately connected to things that lay buried as they are awakened. Seeds germinate when held in dark, rich soil. A child gestates when held in a dark, pulsing womb. Living things speak all the more eloquently for having been held in silence for a time. The Desert Fathers understood this reality—silence is, indeed, the mother of the wisest thoughts.

But speech that proceeds from silence is a hard-won freedom. It comes on the other side of the paralyzing fear of not being heard. To be able to "hold one's peace" until it is right to speak is, I think, a life-long lesson in the Holy Spirit's school of sanctification. I gaze with sympathy upon the now much-yellowed clipping taped into the front of my paternal grandmother's Bible. It begins "Lord, Thou knowest that I am growing older. Keep me from becoming talkative and possessed with the idea that I must express myself on every subject."

This is not to say that we should never initiate speech—such a statement would make silence into a ridiculous law rather than a treasured freedom. Nor should the poison of abusive speech ever be passively swallowed. Here silence is destructive and certainly not initiated by the Spirit's prompting. Godly speech and godly silence are born of a wholesome patience that fear knows nothing about.

In the midst of the spiritual freedom to be silent come the life-giving moments when the quiet bearer of such speech must speak. That voice prays and waits for receptivity's gate to open on the part of the hearer. How do we know when to give voice to this speech that proceeds from silence? My best answer seems embarrassingly simple: we speak when we are invited.

There is some quality in speech born of thoughtful silence that involves an invitation of some sort if is to be well-spoken and well-heard. And while invitations come in many forms, an invitation on the part of the listener offers the speaker this incomparable gift—the lack of any need to strive. Rather, words can be offered with unforced clarity and simplicity. Healing things can go down deep in the hearer, like honey soothing a throat. Hard, but true things can be said without the need to raise one's voice in combat. To be whole, the church needs loving, grounded, wise voices whose words have come from the depths of godly silence.

Such silence proceeds from having made peace with the Lord's purposes when he allows our little ships to stay anchored in the harbor at points when we think we are ready for adventure. Our souls may need to catch up with our longings. Great souls are tried on the high seas but they are not normally formed there. Their foundation is laid as the wind blows the dross from our passions and desires while we are still anchored in the harbor. Our character is formed in the small corners where no one is looking. Jesus didn't begin his ministry until he was thirty. The veil was lifted from his mother's life for a very few moments of the whole. The essence of normal human experience can be painfully unremarkable. Spectacular adventures are the exception.

Where the Spirit of the Lord is, there is freedom to be visible or hidden, handmaidens of the Lord for him to do with as he wills. Not only did Mary not draw attention to herself at the wedding in

Cana, redirecting the servants' attention to Jesus, but after that miracle she had only one more significant appearance to make before she "dissolves in the Church like salt in water."[19] She would stand at the foot of our Lord's cross as he made provision for her. She was visible there, more eloquent in her silence than in any words she could have spoken.

All of this simple freedom is faced with new risks when the context for us to speak or act is drawn out of hiddenness into the bracing winds of the public domain. Here we are not only called to navigate the seas right before us, but to take on the additional perils that come when we embark on an open sea voyage rather than remaining quietly anchored in harbor.

We may, on occasion, find ourselves in high-sea adventures that our souls are not yet ready to handle. I once experienced a brief season where I stepped fairly deeply into the ministry God had given to an older friend and mentor. The context was large and intense, and I found myself overwhelmed at times with the sheer magnitude of the experience. When I attempted to put my disequilibrium into words, I told this friend, "I feel like I have stepped from a canoe paddling down a peaceful river to whitewater rafting." Her thought-provoking response was that my exhilarating experience of rafting had generally been experienced in her life more like the canoe on the river. I gradually realized that my adventure-loving soul needed more time to grow in the shelter of less turbulent waters and eventually stepped back into the quieter season of life I personally had been given.

Between then and now I have received a couple of helpful truths. First, I am not the best evaluator of the treasure deposited within me, or the timing of its offering. The desires of a human heart may be quite genuine, but the soul needed to carry them may need to grow larger. Second, my desires themselves may need to be purified. As reflected upon in "Wisdom," my heart is all too capable of running after my eyes, and the cleansing and ordering of my desires take both time and attentive waiting on the Lord.

There is much to do on these vessels, however, as we wait for the Lord's specific bidding. Our life's voyage may well last a long time, and the point of the expedition is not just making a particular destination. Learning to serve in hidden ways, to love what is put right in front of us—these, again, are the everyday spiritual disciplines of a heart that longs to offer one's particular gift to the world but has not yet been given the specific orders for which we await. We can wait in a spirit of mutiny or a spirit of freedom. We can find ourselves sinking with great regularity or bobbing back to the surface, over and over again. The journey continues either way, but our experience of the passage is radically different.

I was recently invited to submit a short piece to an on-line magazine. I had written a blog entry some time ago that I thought might work and sent it on. They were glad to have it, and it was effortless on my part. But its acceptance engendered an interesting email exchange with one of the editors. I wrote, "One of the ways God consistently works with me is simply to bring me the next thing. I've learned—over and over—that it doesn't work for me to go shopping to find it." And she wrote back,

> I've always felt the same way about God's working in my own life. It's *never* worked to shop around and try to "get." Beth Moore talked about it once, saying "the things we manipulate are seldom ours to keep." I felt as though I was a great manipulator in my life—good at getting things orchestrated and

> getting where *I* wanted to go...The things I've
> tried to get for myself were seldom worth keeping,
> and were seldom things I could hold onto. The
> things he's placed before me have been the
> keepers, the blessings I never saw coming, the
> heart's desires, and always the next step to where
> he was taking me—and where I could never have
> seen for myself. Now I know and I say to him, "I
> only want what you place before me; then I'll
> know it's right."[20]

What freedom is ours when we can simply let the wind blow where it wills and follow where the Spirit is leading us. Because our world thrives on visibility and self-assertion, I do not know of any spiritual discipline that will plow up the ground of our hearts more deeply than renouncing the cultural push toward self-promotion. Of course we read about the guest who takes his place at the head table, only to be asked to take a lower seat. But we don't often act as though Jesus meant what he said.

I can name my chief anxiety in this regard—if I entrust myself to the wind of the Spirit, I will never reach ports of call where I can actually offer the treasure deposited in my hold. The idea of peaceful restraint, whether in speech or in action, taps into a deep-seated fear that if I do not put myself forward my "gifts" will be wasted. I am constantly reminded that it isn't "my" treasure, and that the Holy Spirit responsible for this deposit is not going to forget where he put it.

The patience to take the lower place and wait to be invited forward presupposes hosts and hostesses in Christ's church who make it their responsibility to know the guest list well enough to help members find their authentic place in the whole. Here, again, is where the stable current of the Spirit working within the established means of church structure is intended to be sensitive to the surprising wind blowing over her bow.

Whenever the spiritual eco-system of predictable current and unpredictable wind are separated, the people of God will have the propensity to spin in one of two directions. We may be tempted to mimic the world in our efforts to draw attention to ourselves or else we may withdraw completely out of fear or despair. The treasure carried in our hull will either be plundered before its time or remain undiscovered by the community in which it rests.

The true spiritual eco-system was set into the fabric of creation: God creates. We name. In the garden, God created the living creatures "and brought them to the man to see what he would call them."[21] And when the mother ship is functioning well, this same dynamic is at work in the church. We do not name ourselves. The community names us out of the collective wisdom they have received from above. They call us to love and to serve based on the evidence of what they perceive God to have planted within us by virtue of personality, life experience and the graces born of the Spirit. We live in unity and bless the stirrings of the new thing God is doing in and among us and move forward in love. Have you ever seen a ship in full sail? This is what she looks like in the church. There is nothing more glorious. But it takes a whole crew.

Our Hulls in the Storm

The Secret in Suffering

As billowing sails offer us an opportunity to reflect on our responsiveness to the wind of the Spirit as we navigate through life, the significance of a ship's hull allows us to pause and consider the particular signature of God's grace when the storms of life take their toll on our very human frames. The Apostle Paul is particularly qualified to speak to the strain on our human hulls.

By the time this Apostle had penned his second letter to the church in Corinth, his journey had been anything but easy. Luke amplifies upon the affliction Paul experienced in Asia as he informs us with magnificent restraint, "there arose no little disturbance concerning the Way."[22] A riot had ensued in Ephesus, instigated by greedy and envious merchants who had begun to lose money when people started to turn to the living God and stopped buying their religious wares. Couched in a concern for their goddess, Artemis, these men enraged the crowds, throwing the whole city into confusion as they all rushed together into the theater, dragging Paul's companions with them. Paul wanted to join his friends inside and was only prevented from being thrown to the human lions by disciples and city officials who restrained him from entering the theater. After enduring three hours of fevered chanting to their goddess, a city clerk finally communicated to the crowd that they were in danger of being charged with rioting for no cause. The crowds dispersed, and Paul and his companions left Ephesus soon thereafter.

But the experience took its toll on the Apostle's human frame. Paul tells the Corinthians that he and his companions felt that they "had received the sentence of death."[23] And while he still exalted in the privilege of carrying "the light of the knowledge of the glory of God in the face of Jesus Christ," he says in the next breath, "But we have this treasure in jars of clay to show that the surpassing power belongs to God and not to us."[24]

I find it amazing that the man so uniquely gifted by birth, training, personality and utter transformation of life to be the major architect of Christian theology is so incredibly human. Paul never minimizes what this calling has cost him, while, in the same breath, uttering a kind of sincere, "All right then. The more it hurts, the more Jesus shines through." Paul is buoyant precisely because he knows that he is not invincible.

To know one's self as a human hull or, to use Paul's analogy, a jar of clay, is to be painfully aware of the limitations and frailty of our humanity. Hulls get pretty thin in places through the storms of life. Paul tells us about the beating his hull has taken in no uncertain terms. He has suffered from the storms. Life hurts, he says. And I'm so grateful for his honesty. For as glorious as it is to bear fruit and receive wisdom and grow in confidence in the Lord's power to protect, this life does come with a price tag. To become one who is habitually available to the wind of the Spirit makes us simultaneously more vibrantly alive and more aware of how merely mortal we really are. And suffering goes with the territory of this responsive grace. One is not buoyant because nothing ever affects us. If anything, we probably experience suffering more deeply than we would otherwise because we become more attuned to the sufferings of the world and not merely to our own.

I have a beautiful picture in my office. It is a richly detailed black and white sketch of Jesus with three women. The scene is intimate and somber; it subtly depicts a moment just after Jesus has told his disciples he must go to up to Jerusalem and die. These women are expressing concern and sorrow. One older woman sits to Jesus' right with her fingers laced through his, her serious eyes looking to and through him, while a younger woman looks on from the background with wide-eyed solemnity. Jesus himself is looking intently into the eyes of a third woman whose face remains obscured.

These women remained nameless for me until I was reading Hans Urs Von Balthsar's *Love Alone is Credible*. He notes that Jesus did not ask permission of sinners to die for them, and in fact, it was only a few women who understood at all: Mary, his mother, who lived out her life with a sword millimeters in front of her heart, Mary of Bethany, whose single action of anointing Jesus for his burial was the most grounded act of his entire passion, and Mary Magdalene, who would not abandon Jesus even in death.[25]

In this picture, as startling as it first appears, Jesus is inviting these women to pray for him as they quietly walk alongside him on his lonely road to the cross. Jesus later will redirect the weeping of the women of Jerusalem,[26] but he does not shun the company of the women who have loved him nor does he make any attempt to shield them from his suffering. Could there have been a particular kind of human comfort in their responsive love, and by extension, in their wordless prayers? While these women could not have fully understood the meaning of his suffering, their hearts still beat with his own as they stood with him at the cross, accompanied his body to his burial, and ran to tell the disciples of his resurrection.

Suffering is not to be sought. There have been periods in church history where the propensity of Christians to go looking for suffering was a real problem. When Christians were being martyred for their faith in the early church, the elders made a distinction between bravado—a false confidence in self that would voluntarily throw oneself to the lions—and real courage. Like wisdom, true courage had to be received from above. Those grasping courage's counterfeit were not able to stand. They quickly discovered how fearsome and lonely it was out there, and in the end those who proudly volunteered for martyrdom denied Christ. In contrast, Christians who, while going about their everyday lives, found themselves in situations where they were called upon to suffer and even to die for their faith were blessed with an extraordinary experience of the presence of Jesus right in the midst of their suffering.

Just as suffering is not to be sought, neither is it an end in itself. Paul did not look for a riot in Ephesus, three shipwrecks, or the censure of both Jews and Gentiles. His eyes were fixed on a greater prize, and the finite vessel of his body simply took the beating on the way.

But finally, suffering is not to be run from. As the great spiritual director, Baron Von Hugel, wrote in a letter to his niece, "Suffering is the greatest teacher; the consecrated suffering of one soul teaches another. I think we have got all our values wrong, and suffering is the crown of life."[27] This is an odd concept in a culture that has succeeded in making a visit to the dentist almost as painless as a visit to a spa. But the supreme value of suffering is not odd in God's eyes.

I wonder if the receptive soul's cross to carry is often that of silent, steady suffering with and for others, with and for Christ's church. Called to be Jesus' friends, we are called to share his heart.[28] Like the three Marys we sometimes bear our agony in silence when there is nothing else we can do. We stand, waiting with our healing ointment, ready for the moment when we are freed to move forward again.

Yet, while part of buoyancy's domain is to be present to the suffering of others, sometimes the pain is deeply personal and pierces us through. There are so many kinds of pain. One of the more crippling forms is the emotional and spiritual pain we experience when relationships are torn apart and the enemy sifts our souls like wheat. In these moments, "forgive us our sins as we forgive those who sin against us" becomes the existential cry of those whose relational hulls are gouged and taking in water very fast.

After months of desperately attempting to walk a very difficult situation well, I found myself at a Good Friday service kneeling at the foot of the cross. And while I wanted to focus on Jesus' suffering, I could not see past my own bruised soul. Up till that moment I had labored under the misconception that it was possible in this particular situation to sort out my sin and the sin committed against me. I wanted a two-column balance sheet: the short list of my sin in one and the long list of the sin committed against me in the other, with a nice, clear black line between the two. There was just one problem. As I reached out my hand and touched the cross after so many exhausting months, the clear black line became an indistinguishable smudge across the page. And suddenly, my careful litigation ceased to matter. Jesus was *made* sin—all of it—no columns—my sin against them, their sin against me, our collective sin against others, more collective sin against us. He took it all.

As I touched the cross, this plea rose from my heart: "Lord, please give me a transfusion. Connect the arteries and veins of your great suffering heart to my little one that aches so badly. Lift from me the weight of my sin and the sin committed against me. I release the compulsive need to sort it all out. What I need is the exchange of your life for the living death I am caught in. Lord have mercy." And in the moments that followed, the excruciating pain was lifted from my heart.

I was not an island unto myself in that service. Many of God's people knew of my agony. I have no doubt that they prayed while I wept. But at the foot of the cross and in the midst of God's people, the Lord heard my cry and healed my heart.

I will not say I never ached for the situation again. But I had been met in my suffering and came to understand more deeply the power of Christ on the cross. "Surely he has borne our griefs and carried our sorrows...With his stripes we are healed."[29] The leaky hull of my soul was again made watertight and I did not sink. I had encountered God's abounding grace once again and could take the next waves as they came.

Every human hull suffers at times because the wind is blowing hard and the boat is rocking furiously. In these moments we are to name our distress honestly and entrust ourselves fully to our faithful Creator. The remarkable quality of God's comforting grace is that the ongoing benefits last a lifetime. While we are being hit hard we can often see nothing beyond the next wave. Even so, we are drawn into the eternal deeps of divine love.

Here, then, is the secret of suffering: if we will carry the glory of God in the face of Christ in our little human vessel even as the waves crash hard against us, we will, for the rest of life, carry the incomparable cargo of his comfort in our hulls. And it is not for the sufferer's benefit alone. For anyone who is suffering can quickly perceive the safe harbor of understanding in one who has also suffered. As the Apostle Paul affirmed, "we comfort others with the comfort with which we ourselves are comforted by God."[30]

The Way of Weakness

But there is a second kind of challenge faced by our human hulls on turbulent seas. Paul offers such a graphic picture of this strain upon our human frames: "we have this treasure in jars of clay, to show that the surpassing power belongs to God and not to us."[31]

These finite vessels of ours are really quite fragile. Life's circumstances are hard enough anyway, and we'd prefer to face them with robust resolution. We want to be unsinkable, but, unfortunately, somewhere along the line we discover a rather serious crack or two in our hulls. But God always heals, right? If He would just mend it, we would be so much more confident in our ability to face life's storms. So we ask him to please remove this inhibiting fracture from our lives…and God says, "No, it is good that you are a cracked vessel. I do not choose to mend you. Rather, I will cover your deficiencies with my mighty hand. As long as you remain in me, all will be well."

"But Lord, I'd rather be healed than be held. Wouldn't I be more resilient if I didn't constantly carry this weakness?"…and

God says, "No, I do not want you to be resilient. I want you to be responsive to the slightest wind of my Spirit. As long as you remain sensitive to me, all will be well."

"Lord, I know this is getting old, but are you sure you know what you are doing? I now know how hard the waves can crash. I am not at all confident that the crack won't split wide open at some point. After all, I am just a small boat, and your treasure is weighty and presses deeply against my weakest places." And God says, "Child, I love you. I will never fail you. I will not remove my hand from your cracked hull. But my strength is made perfect in your weakness. Accept this truth and be at peace."

Even as our hearts become habitually available to receive God's word and wisdom, his protection and peace, there are no guarantees that everything we ask for we will receive in the form we desire. The Apostle Paul left us the record of his actual conversation with the Lord concerning his own chronic weakness.[32] But he is not alone in tasting such weakness. Our mentor throughout this book, Mary, also left us her testimony of grace in the midst of weakness. Though wordless, it is no less eloquent.

From the moment that Mary spoke her last word in Cana until she stood at the foot of her son's cross, her encounters with Jesus were one silent "no" after another. She must have felt keenly her weakness as the waves consistently crashed over her heart in the three years of her son's ministry. She daily faced her utter inability to protect him from others. What could she possibly have said the next time she encountered the neighbors who had attempted to throw her son off the cliff?[33] What must it have been like to feed others the food she intended to serve Jesus had her family been successful in bringing him home?[34] There came a point in Mary's life where her words and actions had no apparent impact on the actions of her son. His ever-widening circle of adopted "mothers and brothers" opened a space so expansive that she could find no place to fit within it.[35] Her home would never again be the resting place of this man who boldly declared that he had nowhere to lay his head.[36] The grace that had once utterly filled this singular woman's heart and womb must then have held this little ark tightly in her weakness as she was led on her own lonely journey to her son's cross.

It was dark and cold at 3:00 in the morning, but somehow it matched the state of my heart. I was in my third year of teaching at Wheaton, and I was making a very disturbing discovery—it was becoming increasingly obvious to me that my God-given vocation had very little direct connection to the diploma hanging on my wall. I had been trained as a social scientist. But every class I taught somehow morphed into an adventure in discovering the glory of being a soul filled with the presence of the Living God.

I was confused and afraid. I knew I didn't have the academic credentials for this new path. I hadn't been hired to teach such things. And there was no going back to school for another degree. My patient husband had already put me through a five-year Ph.D. program, and I had a three-year-old son. I was pretty realistic at that point. In the small hours of the night I knew that a professor who made such a radical shift was standing on the rolling deck of a high sea, more likely to fall overboard than survive the storm. I was deeply afraid that I would not be able to stay at Wheaton. (My internal fear was so palpable that, when I was called into an administrator's office the following spring, I was convinced he was going to ask me to leave the college. I was told, instead, that I had been voted Junior Teacher of the Year. But even such a tremendous honor merely postponed my departure for two years.)

As I sat in my study that night I found myself struggling with my own redirected direction. I knew I was leaving my self-initiated career for my God-given vocation. But I was so afraid. What would happen to me? What would this mean for my husband and my son? We had invested a great deal in my education but I could produce no resumé for this new thing God was birthing in me. For the first time in my life I tasted the salt-water of weakness. Tears are a briny sort of drink.

In the dead of that night as I cried out to the Lord, he answered me with a word so clear it might as well have been audible. "Stop looking to your credentials or your institution for your security. I am calling you on a different journey and I will make the way for you. All I ask of you is to listen to me and obey."

During the next few years my worst fears were realized. But in the midst of the painful transitions arose a new awareness. God's hands really were mighty to save, and when he wrapped those hands around my cracked hull he was not going to let go no matter how intense the tempest blew.

As this transitional storm began to abate, I embarked upon the uncharted adventure of navigating within this new vocation. I taught a couple of courses, led a few retreats, spoke at a conference or two. But I was eventually faced with a weakness far more foundational than the lack of a resumé. A situation arose where I was confronted with the inadequacy of my theological moorings. I had always been a "quick study," and I had wanted to believe that I could "retool" without too much difficulty after leaving Wheaton. I loved images and could paint helpful pictures of the soul and her relationship to her God. My cracked hull was not immediately noticeable until the implications of my lack of formal theological training became obvious to me. The deep things were not going to be grasped overnight, and I was going to have to study harder and ponder more deeply than I knew to be possible.

My family and I left on vacation in this midst of my struggle, and for two weeks I sat on the boulders of Lake Superior and cried out to the Lord as I faced my bleak future…but he did not answer me. The only thing I knew to do was to go home and cancel everything I was committed to teach at the moment—at least until I got my theological bearings straight. I went home and began to make phone calls. I canceled one engagement after another…until I reached Robert Webber. I had become acquainted with Bob at Wheaton, and when he left the college to start a new program at Northern Seminary, he asked me to teach in it.

When I got him on the phone, I told him that I did not have the academic qualifications to teach in a seminary and that I was pulling out. And Bob said, "No, you are not. I will walk with you. I will meet with you every week and go over your lectures until you are confident that you are theologically grounded."

My tears fell just as freely that day as they had on a cold winter night five years before, but this time they sprang forth in astonished relief. Apparently my weakness was going to be covered by God's hand in the human form of a passionate, out-of-the-box, historical theologian who would not release me. During the next several years God's hand through Bob's actions on my behalf held my cracked soul together. Now, nearly a decade later, my friend and mentor is with his Lord, yet I continue to taste the fruit of God-initiated grace, mediated through Bob's intervention, that continues to infuse my weakness with life-renewing strength.

Perhaps it is not an accident that I recently encountered a friend with a weakness similar to my own. She, too, is at a critical point in her life. But if the Lord births anything in our souls as we walk out our weakness in his strength, it is bold compassion for others who need God's strength in their weaknesses as well. And so, with ironic joy bubbling up through my own fragile vessel, I found myself saying to her, "I will walk with you..."

Songs of Assent

Over the course of a lifetime, we all find ourselves faced with our own "calamitous annunciations"[37] when God asks us to say "yes" to the impossible. Written into a broken humanity's script are the moments where we are faced with weaknesses we cannot avoid and circumstances over which we have very little control. To say "let it be to me according to your word" in those moments requires a responsiveness to God that we cannot manufacture on our own. It is a gift of grace. This grace is born of God's love coursing in and through our human weakness—whether the frail vessel is a virgin mother, a passionate apostle, or our own little lives.

In these moments all paths to and from any possible "yes" must first pass through the cross where all of our creaturely weakness, barrenness and self-induced complications have already been laid on Jesus. He was drained of the fullness he had been pouring out on our thirsty earth, cut off as a vine from its very source of life, suffered as folly proclaimed her hollow triumph over wisdom, and experienced the destitution of the incarnate "the God who sees" struggling with whether his Father saw him. The most calamitous annunciation the world has ever known was his alone. "Not my will, but thine be done" cost him everything.

In the end, Jesus will win everything. He was made like us so that we could be re-made like him. He left more than his grave clothes behind him in that tomb on Easter morning. Emptiness, fruitlessness, folly, fear, and weakness have all been overcome. Risen, he sent, breathed, restored, commanded, ascended...and fills.

Now every creature that knows herself responsive to God can cry, "Lord, send your Spirit and renew the face of our earth. Fill us with your fullness, plant seeds that will bear fruit in season, be our wisdom, cover us in your protection, pour out your comfort into our hurting hearts, hold us in our weakness." Our God delights to pour out the riches of his abundant grace into our waiting hearts. As we taste of this goodness filling our emptiness and strengthening us in the midst of our weakness, we join our voices with those whose enduring songs of assent draw our own small voices into their great hymns of praise:

He has looked upon the humble estate of his servant:

"My grace is sufficient for you for my power is made perfect in weakness."

He has shown strength with his arm;

I will boast all the more gladly of weaknesses that the power of Christ may rest upon me.

He has exalted those of humble estate and filled the hungry with good things,

For the sake of Christ I am content with weakness.

He who is mighty has done great things for me:

When I am weak, then I am strong.

Holy is his name!

Abounding is his grace!

Endnotes

Introduction

[1] Luke 13:20-21

[2] Josef Pieper, *Only the Lover Sings* (San Francisco: Ignatius Press, 1990), 25.

[3] By defining "feminine" in this manner, I am approaching gender as a symbolic expression of a larger reality that transcends biological or cultural definitions. I find my greatest affinity within the tradition expressed by Getrude von le Forte in *The Eternal Woman* (Milwaukee: The Bruce Publishing Company, 1962) and Alice von Hildebrand in *The Privilege of Being a Woman* (Ave Maria University: Supientia Press, 2004), both of whom locate the symbolic significance of femininity in a fundamental posture of receptivity toward God. However, as a non-Roman Catholic Christian, I am exploring the implications of this deeply incarnational approach to gender without adopting all of the Marian assumptions associated with this tradition.

[4] While I am using "icon" in a more generic sense than the carefully written icons of the Eastern Orthodox tradition, these pictures are also intended to function as a kind of window into the spiritual realities under consideration.

[5] Yves Congars, *I Believe in the Holy Spirit* (New York: Crossword Publishing, 1999), 135.

[6] Hans urs von Balthasar, *Prayer* (New York: Sheed and Ward, 1961), 58.

[7] St. Ambrose (333-397) was the first of the church fathers to draw clear parallels between Eve and Mary in *De institutione virginis*

(c.392). See George H. Tavard, in *Women in Christian Tradition* (Notre Dame: University of Notre Dame Press, 1973), 103.

[8] Norman Nagel, "The Annunciation of Mary" (Sunday School Class presented to St. John Lutheran Church, Wheaton, IL, March 26, 2006).

Simplicity

[1] Matthew 10:29

[2] Matthew 6:26

[3] Psalm 84:3

[4] Thomas DuBay, S.M., *The Evidential Power of Beauty: Science and Theology Meet* (San Francisco: Ignatius Press, 1999), 39.

[5] I am operating within a typological hermeneutic in order to reclaim some of the lost strengths of a "pre-modern" worldview. As professor Thomas Howard writes of this earlier epistemology, 'It is a way of looking at things that goes farther than saying that this is *like* that: It says that *both this and that* are instances of the way things are. The sun pours energy into the earth and the man pours energy into the woman because that is how fruit begins...' [Thomas T. Howard, *Chance or the Dance?* (Wheaton, IL: Harold Shaw, 1969), 17.] Viewed through this richly symbolic set of lenses, men and women again become "epiphanies" of the relationship between creator and all of creation. [Alexander Schmemman, "Sacrament and Symbol" in *For the Life of the World* (Crestwood, NY, St. Vladimir's Press, 1998), 141.]

[6] George Herbert, *The Church*, "Providence" St. 5.

[7] Luke 1:29

[8] John 5:30

[9] John 10:17

[10] Psalm 131

[11] John 14:23

[12] John 15

[13] John 14:27

[14] 1 John 1:1-4

[15] Psalm 63:7

[16] Psalm 126:6

[17] Genesis 3:10

[18] Thomas Merton, *No Man is an Island* (New York: Barnes and Noble Books, 2003), 118.

[19] John 13:8

[20] Mark 8:29-34

[21] Luke 22:33

[22] Luke 22:62

[23] Jeremiah 31:3

[24] Mark 9:24

[25] 1 Kings 17:14

[26] For resources on the nature of misogyny and its healing, see Karl Stern, *The Flight from Woman* (New York: Paragon House, 1985) and Leanne Payne, *Crisis in Masculinity* (Grand Rapids: Baker Books, 1985).

[27] Genesis 3:15

[28] Revelation 12:12

[29] Matthew 14:13-33

[30] *Book of Common Prayer* (New York: Oxford University Press, 1990), 302-303.

Receptivity

[1] Geoffrey W. Bromiley, *Theological Dictionary of the New Testament* "makarios" (Grand Rapids: Eerdmans, 1985), 548.

[2] Luke 11:27

[3] Luke 11:28

[4] Luke 1:42,45

[5] Luke 8:15

[6] This meditation on John 14:20 is part of Leanne Payne's foundational teaching on "practicing the presence of God." See Leanne Payne, *The Healing Presence* (Grand Rapids, MI: Baker Books, 2001).

[7] Patrick Henry Reardon, "Psalm 1" in *Christ in the Psalms* (Ben Lomond, CA: Conciliar Press, 2000), 2.

[8] Isaiah 55; Luke 8

[9] T.S. Eliot, "Burnt Norton" in *Four Quartets* (New York: Harcourt, Inc., 1971), IV.150.

[10] Genesis 1

[11] Exodus 14

[12] Hebrews 4

[13] Hans us von Balthasar, *Prayer* (New York: Sheed and Ward, 1961), 131.

[14] Psalm 29

[15] Luke 24:32

[16] Luke 9

[17] John 7:38

[18] Mark 4:13

[19] John 14:27

[20] John 6:63

[21] Hans urs von Balthasar, *Prayer*, 14-15.

[22] 1 Peter 1:23

[23] Ephesians 2:5

[24] Romans 5:5

[25] Genesis 2:15; John 18:1, 20:15

[26] John 20:19

[27] Revelation 3: 14-20

[28] Psalm 24:9

[29] Emily Elliott, "Thou Didst Leave Thy Throne", 1864.

[30] Phillips Brooks, "O Little Town of Bethlehem", 1867.

[31] John 15:2

[32] Such a Christological reading of the text is completely consistent with a historical Christian interpretation of the Psalms as the prayer book on the lips of the church precisely because these prayers were first found on the lips of Jesus. This approach to the Psalms is clearly articulated by Dietrich Bonhoeffer in *Psalms: The Prayer Book of the Bible* (Minneapolis: Augsburg Press, 1970). In the Gospels we see Jesus entering Jerusalem on Palm

Sunday with Psalm 118 singing in his heart, and hanging on the cross to the somber accompaniment of Psalm 22 and Psalm 31— and perhaps all the verses in between. While the Psalter already had messianic overtones for the Jews who originally penned and sang them, the church now prays these prayers from the far side of Jesus' death and resurrection, where David's royal Son sings these Psalms with and through his church. [See Reggie M. Kidd, *With One Voice: Discovering Christ's Song in our Worship* (Grand Rapids: Baker Book House, 2006).] As St. Augustine wrote, "It hardly ever happens that one would not find in the Psalms the voice of Christ and of the Church..." [St. Augustine, *Enarrationes in Ps 59* in Stanley J. Jaki, *Praying the Psalms: A Commentary* (Grand Rapids, MI: Eerdmans Publishing Company, 2001), 20.] For a rich meditation on a Christological reading of Psalm 1, see Patrick Henry Reardon, *Christ in the Psalms* (Ben Lomond, CA:Conciliar Press, 2000), 2.

[33] Psalm 1:1-3

[34] John 15:5

[35] John 14:20

[36] Matthew 3:8

[37] Matthew 13:24ff

[38] *World English Dictionary*, s.v. "darnel."

[39] Matthew 7:15

[40] Psalm 90:7

[41] Matthew 13:1-23; Luke 8: 4-15

[42] Luke 8:13

[43] Jeremiah 4:3

[44] Psalm 139:23-24

[45] 1 John 1:9

[46] 2 Corinthians 5:17-19

[47] Isaiah 54:2

[48] George Herbert, *The Church Porch*, St. 310.

[49] Dallas Willard, *Renovation of the Heart* (Colorado Springs: NavPress, 2002), 79.

[50] C.S. Lewis, *The Weight of Glory and Other Addresses* (New York: MacMillan, Co. 1980), 18-19.

[51] Luke 8:14

[52] Luke 2:19, 3:51

[53] Luke 8:15

Wisdom

[1] Penelope Duckworth, *Mary: The Imagination of Her Heart* (Cambridge, MA: Cowley Pub., 2004), 23.

[2] James 3:17

[3] Proverbs 1:20

[4] Proverbs 3:15

[5] Proverbs 7:4

[6] Proverbs 9:1

[7] Martin Luther is one of the strongest advocates for Mary as "our dear professor and teacher" through her *Magnificat*. He writes, "This little maid has seen more accurately into the Scriptures than all the Jews, and she had connected with all the

prophecies and examples which are to be found anywhere in Scripture." Her well-digested song contains the heart of God's revealed heart. As Luther continues, "The dear Virgin is occupied with no insignificant thoughts; they come from the first commandment, 'You should fear and love God,' and she sums up the way God rules in one short text, a joyful song for all the lowly. She is a good painter and singer; she sketches God well and sings of him better than anyone, for she names the God who helps the lowly and crushes all that is great and proud. This song lacks nothing; it is well sung, and needs only people who can say yes to it and wait. But such people are few." [David S. Yeago, "The Presence of Mary in the Mystery of the Church" in Carl E. Braaten and Robert W. Jenson, ed., *Mary: Mother of God* (Grand Rapids, MI: Eerdmans Pub., 2004), 77.] Other helpful works in considering the wisdom of Mary's *Magnificat* include Beverly Roberts Gaventa and Cynthia Rigby, ed., *Blessed One: Protestant Perspectives on Mary* (Louisville: Westminster John Knox Press, 2002), and Samuel Terrien, *The Magnificat: Musicians as Biblical Interpreters* (New York: Paulist Press, 1995).

[8] 1 Peter 3:1-6

[9] Proverbs 9:1-6

[10] Revelation 1:20

[11] 1 Peter 2:2

[12] 1 Corinthians 3:2

[13] Matthew 13:52

[14] Proverbs 9:8

[15] Proverbs 9:5

[16] Proverbs 9:6

[17] Proverbs 9:11

[18] "O Come, O Come, Emmanuel" Latin, 12th Century.

[19] Dorothy Sayers, *The Mind of the Maker* (New York: Harper SanFrancisco, 1979), 188.

[20] Proverbs 8:30,31

[21] Luke 2:40

[22] Luke 2:52

[23] Matthew 8:27

[24] Revelation 5:12

[25] Hebrews 7:25

[26] James 1:6

[27] James 1:5

[28] Psalm 90:17

[29] Psalm 19:11

[30] James 3:17-18

[31] Proverbs 2:6-10

[32] James 3:17

[33] Proverbs 9:13-18

[34] Proverbs 9:4,16

[35] J.R.R. Tolkien, *The Lord of the Rings* (Boston: Houghton Mifflin, 1993), 183.

[36] Ibid.,182.

[37] Job 31:7

[38] Josef Pieper, *Living the Truth* (San Francisco: Ignatius Press, 1989), front cover.

[39] Proverbs 9:17

[40] I am, of course, simply describing one of the many prevalent aspects of gnosticism in our day. By describing the dynamics of gnosticism "close to the ground" I want to explore the debilitating nature of this heresy as it wreaks its destruction in unsuspecting lives.

[41] James 3:16

[42] James 3:15

[43] Among the very helpful resources I have consulted in exploring Jesus' sustained interaction with women in the Gospels are the following: Richard Bauckham, *Gospel Women: Studies of the Named Women in the Gospels* (Grand Rapids, MI: Eerdmans, 2002); Margaret M. Beirne, *Women and Men in the Fourth Gospel* (London: T&T Clark International, 2003); Ben Witherington III, *Women in the Ministry of Jesus* (Cambridge University Press, 1984).

[44] Luke 11:4-5

[45] Proverbs 1:7

[46] Proverbs 27:12

[47] T.S. Eliot, "East Coker" in *Four Quartets*, IV.150.

[48] Proverbs 2:4

[49] James 3:13

[50] Proverbs 25:11

[51] T.S. Eliot, "East Coker" in *Four Quartets*, II.90.

Confidence

[1] Luke 2:25-35

[2] Matthew 1:19

[3] Luke 1:56

[4] Matthew 1:13-18

[5] Isaiah 49:11

[6] Luke 2:49

[7] Luke 2:52

[8] Luke 4:29

[9] Matthew 16:24

[10] Romano Guardini, *The Lord* (Washington D.C.: Regnery Pub., 1996), 11.

[11] John 19:27

[12] Isaiah 61:10

[13] 2 Corinthians 5:21

[14] Luke 7:36-50

[15] Ben Witherington III, *Women in the Ministry of Jesus* (Cambridge: Cambridge University Press, 1987), 55-56.

[16] Isaiah 57:15

[17] Genesis 16:13

[18] Luke 7:50

[19] J.R.R. Tolkien, *The Lord of the Rings* (Boston: Houghton Mifflin, 1993), 350.

[20] See Leanne Payne, *The Healing Presence* (Grand Rapids: Baker Books House, 2001).

[21] John 20:31

[22] Luke 10; John 11–12

[23] John 11:17-27

[24] Matthew 16:17-18

[25] John 12:2

[26] John 11:54

[27] Luke 10:41-42

[28] Luke 19:34

[29] John 11:5,6

[30] Genesis 16:6

[31] Genesis 16:13

[32] "[Vulnerability] describes the fundamental openness of the person to being affected by life, persons, and events. To be human is to be vulnerable, subject to the events and persons that affect us for good and ill." Michael Downey, *Altogether Gift: A Trinitarian Spirituality* (Maryknoll, NY: Orbis, 2001), 26.

[33] Psalm 62:5-6

[34] John 4

[35] Mark 5:24-34; Luke 8:42-48

[36] Leviticus 15:25

[37] Luke 5:12

[38] Luke 5:17

[39] Luke 6:6

[40] Luke 7:36

[41] Luke 7:48-50

[42] Luke 8:47

[43] Luke 8:48

[44] Hans urs von Balthasar, *Prayer*, 14.

[45] Matthew 28:20

[46] C.S. Lewis, *Letters to Malcolm: Chiefly on Prayer* (New York: Harcourt, Brace, Jovanovich, 1964), 103.

Buoyancy

[1] Introduction by Alan Villiers in Basil Lubbock, Illustrated by Jack Spurling, *The Best of Sail* (New York: Grossett and Dumlett, 1975).

[2] Pieper, Josef, "Fortitude" in *The Four Cardinal Virtues* (Notre Dame, IN: University of Notre Dame Press, 1966), 12.

[3] Jacob of Serug, *On the Mother of God* tr. Mary Hansbury (Crestwood, NY, Vladimir's Seminary Press, 1998), 19.

[4] St. Cyprian of Carthage, *On the Unity of the Church*, Treatise 1, Part 6.

[5] World Book, 1998, s.v. "Ocean."

[6] John 3:8

[7] Raniero Contalamessa, *Mary: Mirror of the Church* (Collegeville MN: Liturgical Press, 1992), 180-181.

[8] 1 Peter 3:21

[9] *The Best of Sail*, 25.

[10] *Mary, Mirror of the Church*, 181.

[11] Ibid, 181.

[12] 2 Corinthians 9:8

[13] 2 Corinthians 11:24-28

[14] 2 Corinthians 1:8

[15] 2 Corinthians 2:14

[16] 2 Corinthians 3:17

[17] 2 Corinthians 6:8-10

[18] Henri Nouwen, *The Way of the Heart* (New York: Ballatine Books, 1981), 37.

[19] *Mary, Mirror of the Church*, 184.

[20] Email correspondence with Janine Petry, September 12, 2008.

[21] Genesis 2:19

[22] Acts 19:23

[23] 2 Corinthians 1:9

[24] 2 Corinthians 4:7

[25] Hans urs von Balthasar, *Love Alone is Credible* (San Francisco: Ignatius, 2004), 66.

[26] Luke 23:28

[27] Baron F. Von Hugel, *Letters to a Niece* (London: Fount Pub., 1995).

[28] John 15:14

[29] Isaiah 53:4

[30] 2 Corinthians 1:4

[31] 2 Corinthians 4:7

[32] 2 Corinthians 12:8-10

[33] Luke 4:29

[34] Mark 3:21

[35] Mark 3:31-35

[36] Matthew 8:20

[37] T.S. Eliot, "Dry Salvages" in *Four Quartets,* II.60.

Printed in the United States
139814LV00003BA/1/P

9 780578 010236